D0597790

Chasing Warblers

Number Forty
The Corrie Herring Hooks Series

Chasing Warblers

Text by Bob Thornton
Photography by
Vera and Bob Thornton

University of Texas Press
Austin

Printed in China

First edition, 1999

(∞) The paper used in this publication meets the minimum requirements of American National Standard for Information Sciences—Permanence of Paper for Printed Library Materials, ANSI Z39.48-1984.

LIBRARY OF CONGRESS
CATALOGING-IN-PUBLICATION DATA

Thornton, Bob, 1940–
Chasing warblers / text, Bob Thornton ; photography, Vera and Bob Thornton. — 1st ed.
p. cm. — (The Corrie Herring Hooks series ; no. 40)
Includes bibliographical references (p.) and index.
ISBN 0-292-78162-8 (alk. paper)
ISBN 0-292-78163-6 (pbk. : alk. paper)
1. Wood warblers—Migration. 2. Wood Warblers—Migration—Pictorial works. I. Title. II. Series.
QL696.P2438 T48 1999
598.8'721568—dc21 98-25415

WE dedicate this book to the core principles of conservation and to those who are committed to preserving critical habitat so necessary to the health and survival of our American songbirds—like the North American Wood Warblers.

Contents

Photograph Locations

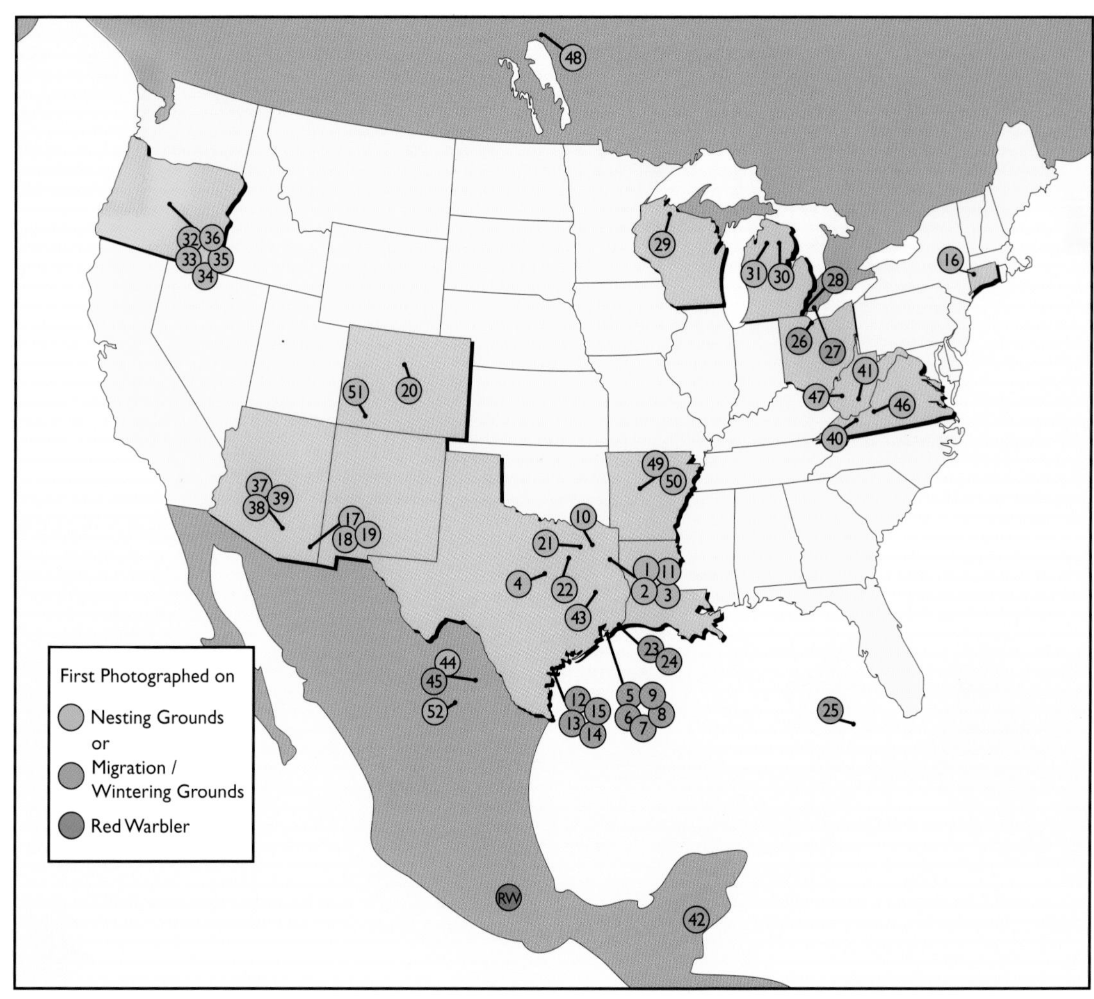

Wood Warblers

THIS book is indeed about wood warblers—small, distinctively patterned songbirds from the tropics that come to the United States but once a year to nest, and are romanticized by many as the "butterflies of the bird world."

The book is also about how Vera and I came to be fascinated by them, were surprised and pleased when we were able to get close enough to photograph a few, and finally undertook a challenge to try to take photographs of them all. That the two of us would be the ones to embark on this kind of adventure is in itself a bit peculiar, since we both grew up in communities noted for things other than the richness and variety of their wildlife—a small West Texas town in Vera's case, the soft suburbs of Dallas in mine. Also perhaps atypically, I was a city banker by profession while Vera's community activities had also been confined to an urban landscape. Along the way we had indeed developed a keen interest in conservation in general and wildlife photography in particular, but had become only modestly knowledgeable in birding itself as we had not pursued the study or purposeful recording of those new species we encountered.

But come to this quest we did, and in so doing we stepped into a special, natural world of spruce bogs and river bottoms and oak ridges, by which we would become enchanted, in pursuit of the different warbler species indigenous to those habitats. While our friends sensibly spent their vacations and holidays in more traditional ways, we chased warblers. While they made elegant attacks on restaurants in Provence, floated dry flies on the Miramichi, or patrolled the manicured greens at Pebble Beach, we found ourselves negotiating more uneven terrain. Our search took us from the dark woods of northern Minnesota, to the eastern slopes of the Cascades in Oregon, and up through the evergreen expanses of New England and Canada. In between, we slogged through Ozark river bottoms in Arkansas, scaled bluffs in the Chiricahuas of Arizona and the Sierra Madre of Mexico, and spent several seasons stalking a variety of different warbler species among the hardwood forests of West Virginia and East Texas.

Additionally, each spring when the songbirds would launch from the Yucatán to fly over the Gulf of Mexico on their annual migration to their northern nesting areas, Vera and I would most likely be waiting for them along the way at one of several ambush points known as "migratory traps." Many a spring weekend morning was spent in such unlikely places as High Island, Texas, or later in the season at Crane Creek, Ohio, or that famous spit of promontory known as Point Pelee, Ontario. This in hopes of catching the birds as they moved through—a bit wearier and lower to the ground, a bit more deliberately feeding, and therefore providing a better opportunity for a close-up photograph of them.

This project was also about people—not only ornithologists but also conservationists, wildlife artists, eco-tour leaders, and other wildlife photographers and writers. There were hard-core birders, soft-core birders, and weekend birders, many of whom were extraordinarily helpful to us in taking time to prelocate a species we were after, assisting with an on-site location, or identifying song variants peculiar to the region.

The real adventure, however, was driven by the birds themselves—the wood warblers, those 4½-inch, multicolored songbirds that come to the United States each spring from Mexico, the Caribbean, and Central and South America to breed. These warblers, along with other species of songbirds such as orioles, tanagers, hummingbirds, and flycatchers, are called "neotropical migrants" since they spend three-fourths of their time each year in the tropics.

Approximately 340 of the 650 total species of birds that nest in the United States are, in fact, designated as "neotropicals." Because these birds are almost exclusively insectivorous, to them migration is not a choice, but an imperative, and when autumn arrives with winter not far behind, most "neotropicals," including warblers, begin heading back south to their tropical homes where their food source is more plentiful and assured. Every country in the neotropics plays winter host to at least some of our nesting U.S. birds. Mexico supports the largest number at over 300; Paraguay the smallest at under 70.

As for the warblers, there are as many as 115 species in the Americas, but Vera and I concentrated on only those that are known to regularly nest in the United States. For the purposes of this project, we did not include those warblers that were either considered to be extinct (e.g., Bachman's) or designated as hybrids (e.g., Brewster's and Lawrence's).

By counting both varieties of Yellow-rumped (Audubon's and Myrtle), along with the Tropical Parula, we set our target at 52. The first was a Prothonotary Warbler, photographed somewhat lackadaisically in 1987 among the cypress and tupelo stands at Caddo Lake, in Texas; the last, a Colima Warbler, taken some nine years later in northern Mexico, after feverish pursuit over three years in two different countries. Although a photograph of record of each of the 52 U.S. warblers was taken in the United States itself, there were several birds, such as the Colima, for which the best photograph was actually taken outside the country.

Warblers are considered special birds by even the hardest-core and most discriminating birders. Tropical bird experts, like John O'Neill and the late Ted Parker, or eco-tour leader Victor Emanuel, seduced regularly by the rainforest magic of quetzals and manakins and cotingas, nevertheless name the wood warbler family as their favorite, and a tree full of migrating warblers as an almost obligatory rite of spring. Even the much admired Eliot Porter, long before he began to specialize in the art of landscape photography that would make him famous, spent most of the first ten years of his career trying to take pictures of as many of the wood warblers as he could.

Why this fascination with warblers? Why the passion for these birds in particular? It may be due to the sheer diversity of their numbers and the varied patterns of their coloration, although there are birds like the tanagers and hummingbirds that are far more strikingly beautiful. Or it could be because of their unusual vocalizations or certain intriguing elements of their behavior, although many members of the wren family, or even our own backyard purple martins, have habits that exceed in interest most anything a warbler might contemplate. This specialness attributed to warblers, however, is most certainly due to their elusiveness; these birds are not that easy to see well, or for very long in any one spot—hence they are appreciated all the more when they are successfully observed. Warblers also, at times, seem to have confiding personalities, and although most scientists would dismiss such a contention as anthropomorphic drivel, many birders nevertheless feel this to be true. Acknowledging that there are specialists who pursue only shorebirds and purists who stand vigil on cold autumn days just to count raptors at Hawk Mountain—when spring winds begin to blow from the south, and a full songbird migration gets under way, most who claim to be birders think "warblers," and denominate the success they have each day by how many of them they see.

But warblers don't really warble. Although warblers are technically songbirds by definition, only a few can stake a claim to having rich, strong voices. They sing, often incessantly, but for the most part they do not sing well. They buzz, chip, and at times sound like insects, making it extremely difficult for most people to recognize and differentiate their songs in the field. Some songs are pitched so high, like the Blackpoll's and the Blackburnian's, that most of us can barely hear them at all. It is said of aging athletes that it's the legs that go first; with birders, it's the high notes. Consequently, the woods are not filled with coveys of old ornithologists tracking Blackpolls by sound. But the Prothonotary's song is nevertheless loud and sharp; the Prairie's one of the busiest; and those of the Louisiana Waterthrush and the Swainson's two of the most musical.

Just as the perfume business has its world-class "nose," and the wine industry its star "taster," birders of this generation for years looked to the late Ted Parker as the acknowledged genius of field ornithologists, especially within the context of recognizing bird sounds. He could not only easily differentiate between all the different warbler songs and call notes with great ease; he had also imprinted the songs of some 4,000 other birds worldwide. It is reported that on one occasion in some obscure rainforest in Central America he even identified the song of an especially rare bird that he had neither heard nor seen before, simply because he knew by elimination what it had to be.

Clearly and accurately identifying the different sounds of warblers and unerringly tracking to the source of their song is critically important to getting close enough to the bird for a decent photograph. Young musicians are predictably good at this; veteran artillery officers aren't. That my own hearing was not all that impressive was something of an issue; that Vera's was remarkably sharp served on many occasions to save the day. I could usually hear the bird well enough, and also more times than not accurately identify it, but my own sense of direction as to locating its source point seemed to be 10–15 degrees off, which was quite simply the difference between finding the bird and impotently stumbling around in a circle looking for it. Vera, however, was always on point, and could head right for the bird every time, with me usually tagging along behind.

Moreover, the names of many of the warblers can be misleading, as many were named for the locales where they were first discovered, often during migration, and bear no relevance to the preferred habitat of the particular bird or its native nesting area. This leads to some surprising contradictions such as Connecticut Warblers not nesting or being found anywhere near Connecticut, nor Cape Mays in New Jersey, nor Tennessees in that state. You can, however, find nesting Kentucky Warblers in Kentucky and Canada Warblers in Canada. Similarly, the name confusion extends to the fact that you won't encounter Prairie Warblers on the Great Plains, nor find Palm Warblers in palm trees. But both Waterthrushes are found near water, and Pine Warblers do indeed nest and feed almost exclusively in pine trees. Furthermore, many of the birds were named for noted ornithologists of the day—Bachman, Wilson, Brewster, Audubon. Consequently, with the exception of color (Black-and-white, Golden-winged, Bay-breasted, Cerulean), the warbler name is of no help either in their specific identification or in the recognition of the habitat in which they can be found.

Nesting warblers can be located throughout the United States, although their density is probably the greatest in the Northeast, where the total mass of warblers in the spring and summer will exceed that of all other birds combined. Vera and I chased them throughout this country, Canada, and Mexico, first during migration and then on their nesting grounds. Our yearly chase would essentially begin the last week in March when the Golden-cheeked would move into the ash juniper and oak Hill Country of Central Texas, being one of the first of the songbirds to return from the tropics. We would usually spend the next three weekends at either Sabine Woods, High Island, or Matagorda Island to intercept the birds after they had crossed the Gulf of Mexico from the tropics to begin the land leg of their northern migration. Old-timers will say that the migration is in full swing across the Gulf when the Rose-breasted Grosbeak is seen, and this occurs about mid-April each year. At that time the number of migrating neotropical species might top 200—with buntings, tanagers, flycatchers, hummingbirds, orioles, as well as warblers making the trip.

Prior to their 600-mile flight across the Gulf, the birds form staging areas in Mexico and the Caribbean, at times grouping by species. From here they launch their night flight about sunset to ride southerly tail winds across the water to the coastal mainland—then on to Ohio, or Maine, or Arkansas, or wherever, to nest. Millions and millions of birds cross over each night that the weather is suitable, and experts with technologically advanced sound-tracking equipment can at times measure the number and species of flock movements by recording and identifying the call notes the birds make during flight. If things go "as planned" and southerly winds prevail, the birds will easily cross the Gulf in 15 hours or so and blow deeply inland the next day before sitting down for the first time to rest. That's great for the birds, but not so rewarding for the birders and photographers crouched on the Texas coast hoping for a closer view.

However, if these birds, having passed the point of no return out over the Gulf, should unexpectedly hit northerly winds with rain, they become exhausted by the time they hit the mainland and drop from the sky to the first place they can find to rest and refuel. On the marshy coastal plains of Texas there are only a few pieces of acceptable habitat for many miles around where the birds can suitably rest and feed. One of these special spots is High Island, Texas—as much a springtime mecca to birders worldwide as Augusta is to golfers during the week of The Masters. What makes this locale so exceptional is a peculiar quirk of geology in the form of a salt dome that uplifts the terrain about 15 feet above sea level. This protects from saltwater oak mottes with 300- to 400-year-old trees—the only such trees for tens of miles in each direction, and a coveted sanctuary and life-saving refuge for these desperate and exhausted survivors of the Gulf crossing. When the birds finally battle through the north winds and rain to reach land and then drop from the sky into these oak mottes, the event is hailed as a "fallout" and represents one of the most dramatic wildlife spectacles in this country. Species after species, bird after bird, spiral down from the sky into the trees, bushes, and even onto the ground below, with splashes of reds and yellows and blues, spot-painting the foliage like holiday ornaments. This at times permits an approach of several feet to a particular bird that one might have only previously seen at the top of some tall tree or admired from the pages of a Peterson field guide. People from all over the world make pilgrimages each spring to High Island with hopes of encountering one of these special fallout events, although the magnificence of the occasion is diminished by the knowledge that many thousands of the birds crossing the Gulf do not make it. Even though full fallouts occur probably no more than once every couple of years, there is nevertheless a steady stream of overall bird activity on the Texas coast throughout April and early May. This represented an important opportunity for Vera and me to get close to some of our targeted warblers, many of which would otherwise feed and nest too high for close viewing, much less suitable photography.

Many of the warblers we photographed, and nearly all of the spruce warblers of New England and Canada, we captured at the migratory traps on the Texas Gulf Coast, the Dry Tortugas off the Florida Keys, or at Point Pelee and Crane Creek on opposite sides of Lake Erie. Correct positioning for spring migration was a linchpin in our strategy to photograph these birds, although this tactic was applicable only to those warblers that were coming to nest in the East, Midwest, and North and were using flyways over the Gulf of Mexico. Western warblers, which winter for the most part in western Mexico and Central America, migrate northward over land in the spring and avoid the long water crossings. Consequently, we were forced to develop a completely different strategy for those western birds. Also, trying to photograph warblers during fall migration when they were drifting southward back home toward the tropics didn't work well for several reasons. The birds were scattered as opposed to being concentrated, and since they were preparing to cross the Gulf going the other way, they weren't weary on the U.S. side of the water. Moreover, by then many of the birds had molted into their dull fall plumage, having shed their brilliant breeding colors of spring, and were thus unacceptably lackluster by comparison for photography purposes.

It is fascinating to most, and one of the true wildlife wonders of nature, that the migration imperative evolved as it did. Like other songbirds, the warblers come to the temperate zone to breed when our U.S. and Canadian springtimes see an explosion of insect activity and while in certain latitudes there are as many as 50 percent more daylight hours to feed baby birds. Migration itself has created different habits among migratory birds, and those songbirds that migrate to the United States, for example, have larger clutch sizes in anticipation of the heavy toll the very act of migration will have on the species. Unlike geese, swans, and cranes, which initiate their young to migration by flying with them on their first fall trip south and then escorting them back north the following spring, songbirds such as warblers aren't led or taught. Only a special "program" encoded somewhere deep in the fabric of their genes serves to propel them. Migrants also have weaker pair bonds compared to their stay-at-home tropical counterparts and tend to pair up only on their nesting grounds. Additionally, while male and female nonmigrating warblers are most likely to have the same plumage, greater differentiation of plumage exists between male and female migrating warblers. Consequently, Ceruleans and Black-throated Blues will have marked color differences by gender, while those essentially tropical warblers that pioneer but a short way up to the northern boundary of their range into South Texas and southeastern Arizona (like the Painted Redstart, Colima Warbler, Red-faced Warbler, and Tropical Parula) have no appreciable color differences between male and female at all.

Although through the 1980s we had taken pictures of a couple of warblers on their nesting grounds in East Texas, and had been initially successful with migrating birds crossing the Gulf, we nevertheless had crafted no real plan for trying to photograph all of these birds. We were thereby forced to more or less make one up as we went along. Although the project itself spanned a nine-year time frame, we were only active at it a few weeks each year during the spring nesting season when the birds were the most vibrant in their breeding plumage.

As to our equipment, we were in pretty good shape, as we had taken the advice of Sid Rucker, the accomplished wildlife photographer, who early on had shamed us away from some fairly ancient and limiting gear into a modern generation of Nikon equipment which we found to be entirely suitable for our purposes. The real key to our photographing a constantly moving bird like a warbler was a relatively slow Nikon 300-f4, which could be hand-held since it was light and maneuverable. Most professional wildlife photographers we knew swore by their big, fast 300-f2.8s or 400-f4s as their basic gear, along with 1.4 or 2.0 converters. This larger, faster equipment did have real light and magnification advantages, but its extra weight tended to weld the photographer to the tripod, thereby constricting the maneuverability we felt was necessary for chasing small birds through thick brush. Californian Brian Small, however, swears by his monster 500 setup, and his songbird photographs are as good as they get. Additionally, professional photographers like Arthur Morris, Barth Schorre, Paul Konrad, and the Maslowski family of Ohio have made big lenses work for them on songbirds with magnificent, artistic results. But Vera and I had decided early on to sacrifice some of the advantages that big, fast lenses offered in order to try to work closer to our targets with lighter gear. Our pictures were taken with full flash, and more often than not within 15 feet of the bird. The flash was essential to our overcoming the persistent obstacles of both movement and the shadows through which the warblers habitually flitted, and provided us with the necessary speed to freeze the action. As to film, we had experimented with several varieties early on, but toward the end of the project had settled on Fuji Sensia 100, which we pushed to 200 with highly acceptable results.

As to photographing these small, elusive birds, we faced several challenges: First, to maneuver within 12 to 15 feet of each warbler. This was tough—at least it was for us. Second, to take a picture that was in sharp focus. This was also hard to do, as a warbler is always in perpetual motion—darting and weaving, ducking and fluttering, in and out of brush and shadows and leaves and such. They are never still. Additionally, in order to confiscate as much light as possible, we shot the camera close to "wide open," leaving no room for any focusing miscalibration and the concomitant "soft shot," which is the devil's curse of all wildlife photographers. "Tack sharp" was what we were always after, but it was not all that easy to come by.

Our third challenge was to take the photograph with enough warm, ambient light to create a reasonably artistic product, as opposed to something that looked textbook-clinical, shot in the dark. This at times presented its own problems since many of the birds preferred the shadows of dark ravines and river bottoms, and even with a flash we found it difficult to consistently flatter them with adequate light. Finally, we needed to capture the most colorful specimen we could find. With but a couple of exceptions, this meant a handsome, mature male in full spring breeding plumage.

The excitement of the quest and the thrill of the chase in our pursuit of warblers was not entirely dissimilar from wild-game hunting itself. Both require proper equipment preparation, knowledge of both habits and habitat, accomplished stalking skills, as well as the ability to focus and "fire" properly. Although a few of our big-game hunting friends, with trophy rooms full of water buffalo, leopards, bongos, and such, were inclined to disparage the stalking of a half-ounce puff of feathers as being a bit "delicate," the similarities were nevertheless real.

The early wildlife photographers who began to concentrate on warblers in the 1950s were limited by the equipment available to them at the time, and they were forced to structure their strategies and techniques around incredible fieldwork skills. They spent what at times were days trying to find a particular bird's nest, and then would set up their cameras and flash equipment and triggering devices at the site. The acknowledged dean of this early effort was Eliot Porter, who during the 1960s and '70s (before he concentrated on color landscape photography) focused his craft on birds in general and warblers in particular. He was substantially assisted by his close friends Powell and Betty Darling Cottrille of Jackson, Michigan, both excellent naturalists and wildlife photographers, as well as Ron Austing, the accomplished photographer from Indiana. These pioneers, along with Hal Harrison, the respected author of *Wood Warblers' World,* had great success with their nest-finding strategies. Their techniques had some marked advantages in that these photographers could always control their light exposures and shoot full depth-of-field with large format lenses, thereby assuring sharp images. Most of Eliot Porter's pictures of warblers are classics, acknowledged works of art. Today his entire collection of songbird transparencies and photographs are preserved at the renowned Amon Carter Museum in Ft. Worth, and include 42 different species of warblers.

But there were also some trade-offs, some clear drawbacks. First and foremost, one had to be able to find the nest and get close to it. This took talent—and lots and lots of time. Some of the nests were extremely difficult to find, and some were also high and obscured from clear view. Another very real, but less obvious problem was that some of the males were not consistent nest feeders, so one could then only succeed in getting a shot of the less colorful female. From a purely artistic standpoint, there was an additional negative in that this kind of photograph invariably included a nest shot of the babies with their mouths agape, not because the photographer necessarily thought the babies were all that fetchingly cute, but simply because that was the only way he could consistently get a chance to photograph one of the parents, preferably the male. Too many quite excellent pictures of beautiful adult warblers were flawed in overall artistic composition by "closet" backgrounds, and a brown nest of twigs full of baby birds. Using this method, however, frequently produced some quite excellent pictures of warblers, but it was tough to get all of the species this way because of the high-nesting birds. Porter wasn't able to, the Cottrilles didn't, and Hal Harrison acknowledged that he couldn't either. There are most likely others who have taken photographs of all of the warblers in the United States, but it is highly doubtful that they have done so by locating the nest of each species first.

Vera and I approached the task with a different spin, and we did not rely on finding nests at all, although we did in fact find a few and got some reasonably good photographs from doing so. We built our strategy first around finding as many warblers as possible on springtime migration routes, tired after they had just crossed a large body of water. We picked up about 20 this way. We were also able to get about 10 more of our warblers on their singing perches or near their nesting sites while foraging or feeding their young. Most of the East Texas birds and some Arizona and Colorado warblers were taken in this manner. For the balance, however, some 20 or so, we relied on tapes of a singing male, fashioned for us by Greg Budney at Cornell's renowned Laboratory of Natural Sounds. By first hearing and then recognizing the song of a particular warbler on its nesting territory, Vera and I were at times successful in getting close to a singing male on his nesting grounds by playing the tape of his song back to him, which he interpreted to be that of an intruding competitor. Hormonal activity would then engage, the territorial drive would kick in, and if we were lucky, the targeted male would flash in for a closer look at his "rival." At times he would come in just close enough to where we were hiding to afford us a reasonably good opportunity for a photograph.

It didn't always work, and with some species it never worked. Even when it did, we found that we needed to play the tape with but a tweak in order merely to pique the interest of the resident male and not harass him with constant playing that would have inevitably caused him to be jumpier and more nervous than usual, and thereby more apt to avoid the source of the sound entirely. This restrained use of tape tactics was also compatible with the American Birding Association's own code of ethics, which decrees only the "sparing use of recordings" and "never in heavily birded areas." Having said this, there were birds we would simply not have gotten without the use of the tape, and a few we just barely got that way at all. Those birds for which the tapes made a real difference were high-nesting western warblers that do not migrate in the springtime over a large body of water (which thus prevented us from more easily capturing them that way).

Another somewhat less intrusive technique, first taught to us by Jim Peterson, then head of ornithology at the Dallas Museum of Natural History, was that of "pishing." "Pishing" is the sound one makes with a series of "p-shhhhs," emphatically delivered, which more or less resembles a scolding wren upset at some intruder. As faintly comical and absurd as this first seemed to us, it nevertheless proved to be remarkably effective in luring furtive songbirds, namely warblers, from the thick brush trying to determine what the fuss was all about. Some warblers responded to "pishing" better than others, the Prothonotary in our experience being the most consistent responder of all. And a curious Wilson's, sneaking close from some heavy reeds near Vail, Colorado, one June morning, provided us with the only acceptable photograph we were ever able to manage of that bird.

Prothonotary Warbler (1), Caddo Lake, Texas, 1987

Swamp Canaries and Caddo

TAKING photographs of all the U.S. nesting wood warblers was not acknowledged by us to be any sort of "project" until some point well along the way, after we had already taken a few. Bird no. 1 thus was not at the time considered to be the first leg of any long race, but was simply a magnificent, small, yellow bird we photographed during a time we were spending weekends at Caddo Lake, near the small East Texas town of Jefferson. The year was 1987 and bird no. 1 was a Prothonotary Warbler.

Jefferson itself is a historic town; in the late 1860s it was one of the largest and most famous port cities in the state. It was perched on the Texas end of Cypress Bayou and served as a gateway for paddlewheel steamers loaded with cotton trying to make their way down the Bayou to the Red River, and then on to the New Orleans marketplace. That is until 1872 when the U.S. Army Corps of Engineers used dynamite to blow up a massive logjam on the Red River, sucking all of the water out of Cypress Bayou. This land-locked Jefferson forever and drove this once proud community into relative obscurity, until nearly a century later it began to claw its way back as a tourist destination due to its charm and natural beauty. It was in Jefferson that Vera and I first asked directions to Caddo Lake, which was to become the focal point of the early part of this adventure and clearly one of the most mysteriously beautiful and enchanting places in the South. Caddo, situated on the Louisiana-Texas border, is the largest natural lake in Texas. Water tupelo and bald cypress trees stand shoulder to shoulder throughout the lake covered with swaying Spanish moss, giving Caddo an almost primeval look. Vera and I saw it for the first time from the end of a pier at the rustic Pine Needle Lodge, which would serve as a useful retreat for us over the following several years as we tried to learn this business of wildlife photography. In regard to that first spring, although there was no focused project yet in mind, Vera and I made certain adjustments necessary for a successful working partnership. As we began our first exploratory canoe ride through the cypress swamps in search of wildlife to photograph, I positioned myself in the front of the canoe with my old Pentax camera and potato-masher flash, with Vera in the stern, dutifully paddling and taking crisp command orders from the bow. This system proved to be reasonably successful, but was operative only that first weekend, as it was fine-tuned on our next outing with Vera commanding the front of the boat with a new camera, and me in the back with the old gear and the paddle. That has more or less been the structure and tone of the arrangement since.

Many an afternoon was spent that first year paddling through the cypress and tupelo stands looking for birds and alligators and other forms of wildlife to photograph. Then one afternoon, in what turned out to be pretty good light, we spotted this dash of bobbing gold,

Prothonotary Warbler, Sabine Woods, Texas, 1996

SWAMP CANARIES AND CADDO

Prothonotary Warbler, Caddo Lake, Texas, 1993

darting from cypress knee to log to stump, moving ever closer to us as it deliberately fed. It was a bird that the locals referred to as "swamp canary"—to us a Prothonotary Warbler. As it darted near where we were holding, we squeezed off a shot and got a surprisingly good picture of what would turn out to be warbler no. 1.

Eight years later, in April 1996, not far from the big refinery complex at Port Arthur, Texas, Vera and I had another spectacular encounter with this bird at a small wooded area, studded with ancient oaks, named Sabine Woods. A nasty cold front with driving rains had swept the Texas coast the night before, and slammed into a wave of early-migrant songbirds crossing the Gulf that evening. What we experienced the next morning was by any measure extraordinary—a fallout of Prothonotary Warblers! They were everywhere, and we estimated that there were easily more than 100 in a confined three-acre area. All of them were on the forest floor, literally at our feet, desperately feeding on insects to renourish themselves. At one point we counted 15 Prothonotaries on the ground within a 10-yard radius from where we were standing. They were tired, tame, and deliberately focused on finding food; and had we been so inclined, we could have scooped them up one by one with a small fishing net and had our limit within 15 minutes. A grizzled old veteran of Sabine Pass, with whom we briefly visited that morning, said that he had been living on the Texas coast for 30 years, and had never seen that many Prothonotaries at any one time. Vera and I also noticed that more than just a few seemed to be in pairs, giving some credence to those who have insisted that this particular warbler does, in fact, occasionally form pair-bonds on its wintering grounds prior to migration. It was a special morning, as the Prothonotaries frenetically worked the understory, bobbing arhythmically like yellow corks on a choppy, dark green sea. This particular bird had been the very first warbler Vera had ever seen, the first one the two of us had ever photographed, and clearly Vera's favorite long before this fallout morning. Consequently, this experience, coming some eight years later toward the end of our search, was particularly thrilling for her.

The Prothonotary is a regular inhabitant of our southern swamps and bottomlands and over time has extended its range throughout the Midwest all the way up to the lower peninsula of Michigan. Whenever you encounter swampy habitat in this broad geographic range, and the time of year is right, you have an opportunity to find this bird. The Prothonotary is also a bit unusual in that it is only one of two warblers that builds its nest in a tree cavity rather than in a tree itself or on the ground (the Lucy's being the other). It prefers a hole in old cypress trees, out over water if possible, to afford it a bit more protection from predators. It is also said that baby Prothonotaries know how to swim, but Vera and I were never fortunate enough to observe that. Nevertheless, the image of this small bird of gold weaving through the dark shadows of the Caddo cypress stands made an indelible imprint on our entire warbler experience.

At the end of the pier at Pine Needle Lodge there is a night-light attached to an old cypress tree that collected a large number of insects each evening, some of which were still around at dawn. This provided many of the songbirds of the area an early morning breakfast, which was also for some the first event of the day. From time to time it was the first event of our day too, as we tried to ambush the birds as they swept in for their morning run. We were able to conceal ourselves under the eaves of the boat-slip's roof, and one spring morning in 1988, we were successful in getting close enough to a Yellow-throated Warbler to take an acceptable photograph. As it turned out, it was warbler no. 2.

Yellow-throated Warbler (2), Caddo Lake, Texas, 1988

The Yellow-throated Warbler is a handsome bird of the pine forests and river bottoms of the South, and ranges all the way through the Carolina low country up through Pennsylvania. West of the Alleghenies the bird is known as the "Sycamore Warbler," and prefers that habitat. Its behavior is unusual in that it patrols the vertical surfaces of a tree very much as a woodcreeper does, and it uses its extremely long and narrow beak to probe bark and pine cones for food. In fact, the Yellow-throated has the longest beak of any of the wood warblers. Vera and I have always liked this bird because of the beauty of its plumage and the characteristics of its song. In addition to taking its picture at Caddo, we frequently encountered the Yellow-throated on migration at Matagorda Island, and some of our best shots of it were actually taken there. It is also worth noting that as we experimented with tapes to call up reluctant and high-feeding birds, the Yellow-throated Warblers proved to be inadequate responders, and we were never able to lure even a one in close enough to do us any good. As a result, we had to content ourselves with those we could approach closely while they were busy feeding, either on their nesting grounds or on migration.

Also at Caddo Lake that same year, Vera and I jumped a pair of Northern Parulas (no. 3) feeding fledglings late one June afternoon as they bounced from red maple to cypress to tupelo on a little bridge that connects the small Caddo community of Uncertain to a water-edged peninsula. We took good pictures that day as both the male and female Parulas would allow us to get right up to them, so thoroughly absorbed were they in the feeding process. We would consistently find Parulas on this bridge and on the docks near a public boat launch some

Yellow-throated Warbler, Matagorda Island, Texas, 1992

Northern Parula (3), near Uncertain, Texas, 1988

Northern Parula, Caddo Lake, Texas, 1991

200 yards away, and these "honey holes" produced Parulas for us over several years.

The Northern Parulas are among our very smallest warblers at about 3 ½ inches long. This required Vera and me to get within 10–12 feet of them to take any kind of meaningful shot since our 300-mm lens, despite the 1.4 converter, was especially limiting for a bird this small. However, this warbler is most confiding, not timid at all, and is as easy to approach closely as any of the warblers we sought. The Parula has an olive saddlepatch on its blue-gray back, and the most striking males also have a full chestnut band across their breasts. The range of the Parula is impressive and runs from the eastern Texas hardwood forests to as far north as New England and southern Canada. In the South, the Parulas will nest exclusively in Spanish moss, hence their attraction to Caddo Lake; and in the North, they will similarly and just as particularly seek out usnea lichen for the same purpose. The Parula's song is buzzy, with a high-pitched, sharp ending, and we would usually hear it long before we saw the bird. Our encounters with it were usually on its nesting grounds, since the spring migration of the Parula is extremely early—late March on the Texas coast—and Vera and I were never quite in place to see it there at that time.

We were pleased with our success with the Parula that particular day, and we celebrated with what had become our regular Saturday-night dinner at the Big Pines Lodge. Snuggled up to the water's edge of Cypress Bayou, Big Pines is more than just a local restaurant; it is a Caddo institution, a big roadhouse on the water that serves to safeguard the integrity of this special lake. The owners, George and Betty Williamson, have stood watch over Caddo for nearly 25 years and have led many efforts to preserve its uniqueness and beauty, and to protect the lake from those who would try to do it harm for economic gain. Big Pines is patronized by a predominantly local crowd that enjoys a jukebox with music that ranges from Glenn Miller and Roy Rogers to the University of Texas Longhorn Band to the latest hits by George Strait, Alabama, and Billy Ray Cyrus. Also, the merchandise for sale at Big Pines is an odd mix—from old fishing lures, to new handguns, to some of the best catfish and jalapeño hush puppies in East Texas. It was the latter that always brought us back when this warbler-chasing business carried us near the little town of Uncertain and those special birds of Caddo Lake.

The Texas Bird

DURING the late 1980s Vera and I spent a lot of spring and early summer weekends in East Texas taking pictures of whatever wildlife we could get close to, be it herons or egrets or summer tanagers or, in fact, most anything that moved. We also began to sample the rainforests of the tropics. On the advice of our friend, Andy Sansom, now director of the Texas Parks and Wildlife Department, we went to Costa Rica in 1987 to photograph the quetzals in the cloud forests of Monteverde and the manakins on their leks in the Caribbean lowlands at La Selva.

On that first trip to Costa Rica we bumped into a lanky and intensely engaging Texan from Austin who introduced himself to us as Larry Gilbert. Larry was chairman of the Department of Zoology at the University of Texas, and was on his way to a research station he had built in a remote area of the Osa Peninsula called Corcovado. Vera and I would spend a week there the following year, but our most unusual tropical experience involving Larry didn't occur in Central America at all, but rather in Austin itself. Vera and I were having dinner with Larry and his wife one night during the winter of 1988 when he invited us to come by the next day to see his "butterfly collection." We agreed, but with that certain, spongy apathy usually reserved for those things one is not all that excited about doing, but feels committed to nevertheless. After all, to us "butterfly collection" meant several encased displays of mounted insects hanging on some den wall. Not so. Larry bypassed his home the next morning, and took us to the top of the roof of the zoology building where he worked, square in the heart of the University of Texas campus. And it was there, on an icy December morning, that we saw Larry's collection—seven greenhouses filled with 120 different species of plants, all covered with butterflies. Live ones. And

Golden-cheeked Warbler (4), Meridian, Texas, 1989

they were flying all over the place. Larry had a collection all right—he raised tropical butterflies from Costa Rica and other rainforest countries of Central and South America, and he was currently working with 14 different species of brightly colored butterflies from the neotropics. On this dull gray roof on this dull gray day in Austin, Texas, there were more than 1,500 different butterflies lighting up the greenhouses with their brilliance. Rainforest color where you would least expect it!

Only a few miles west of campus and Larry's butterfly greenhouses there exists a geological upshift of terrain known as the Balcones Escarpment, which represents a range of habitat for a certain bird that nests exclusively in Texas—the Golden-cheeked Warbler (no. 4). We set out in the spring of 1989 to see if we could find this warbler and take its picture. Finding one proved easy in Meridian State Park in Bosque County about one and a half hours south of Dallas. Photographing it was a completely different story, as it took us nearly three seasons to do so. Warren Pulich of the University of Dallas, who wrote an authoritative work on the Golden-cheeked back in 1976, gave us decent directions, and only 30 minutes into our search one late-March morning we heard one sing. Then we saw it, at the top of an ash juniper (called cedar in Texas) about 25 feet high, marking its territory with a distinctively buzzy song that ended in a short trill. While the bird was much too far back in the brush for any kind of photograph, we were nevertheless delighted that we had finally seen this warbler we had heard so much about. Although there are two other warblers that make their only U.S. nest in Texas—the Colima and the Tropical Parula—these other two birds also nest extensively in Mexico. The Golden-cheeked, however, does not. It nests exclusively in Texas, and the only place on the planet you can find this warbler during the spring of any year is among the cedar/oak canyons of the Texas Hill Country. Although the mockingbird is officially the State Bird of Texas, the Golden-cheeked has established its own compelling credentials for such a designation.

The Golden-cheeked Warbler is a relative of the Black-throated Green of the spruce forests of New England, the Black-throated Gray of the juniper and oak hillsides of the West, the Hermit of Northern California and Oregon, and the Townsend's whose range runs from Oregon to Alaska. All of these birds are distinctively patterned in various combinations of black and white and yellow, and all have songs with predominantly buzzy qualities. The female Golden-cheeked has backed herself into an ecological corner as she will only make her nest from the bark of old cedar, and suitable habitat has to be sprinkled with oak for insect feeding and territorial singing. This has created real problems for the bird since a significant growth corridor of Austin in Travis County points west through the warbler's remaining habitat in this area, threatening its survival there. Consequently, the bird has been placed on the Endangered Species List, which listing served to thrust the warbler into a state of infamy as development during the 1980s in west Travis County came to a complete standstill. In a saga played out time and again, environmentalists were pitted against developers, not unlike the early range wars with cattlemen fighting sheepmen, and the Golden-cheeked was branded the "spotted owl of the Hill Country." Into this fray rode the Nature Conservancy of Texas, which skillfully fashioned a compromise plan among the business community, developers, city officials, and environmentalists to set aside enough critical habitat for the species to survive in the region, thereby permitting the development of remaining acreage to sustain Austin's growth westward. Some of the land saved was bought and then donated by the developers themselves, who were then guaranteed uncontested development of suitable acreage elsewhere in Travis County. The agreement was called the Balcones Canyonland Conservation Plan, and the hope was that it would serve as a model for reconciling the inevitable conflicts between habitat preservation and population growth in the future.

But habitat destruction is not the only threat to the Golden-cheeked. This warbler is also plagued by another bird, a brood parasite, that puts her own eggs in the nest of the Golden-cheeked to the detriment of the baby Golden-cheekeds, which more times than not don't survive. The villain is known as the Brown-headed Cowbird, a serious threat to many songbird populations across the country. The cowbirds historically followed the bison herds that migrated across the western plains feeding on the insects these big animals kicked up. When it was time to nest, the cowbirds couldn't afford to abandon their "movable feast," so they simply laid their eggs in another bird's nest and kept on moving themselves. When cattle replaced the bison on the prairies, the cowbirds adapted easily enough, hence the name. However, when cattle were eventually introduced to areas where the buffalo had not roamed, the resident songbirds of these areas had not evolved defenses against the cowbirds and the environmental balance was thus upset. One of the more disturbing sights in nature is to see a small mother warbler feeding a much larger, begging baby cowbird, which the little warbler is hormonally compelled to nurture as its own. This occurs despite the fact that the cowbird nestling may have just kicked out of the nest the mother's own offspring. Places that Vera and I explored in Travis County were crowded with cowbird populations, but there were also signs of human counterattack evidenced by occasional cages filled with trapped cowbirds earmarked for removal from the area.

We spent several seasons at Meridian State Park trying to get close enough to the Golden-cheeked for a good picture, and although we consistently found the birds, we were not successful for some time in photographing one. We were precluded from playing a tape of the adult male because of the bird's recent placement on the Endangered Species List; tape-playing was technically interpreted to be a form of harassment, and consequently was considered illegal. Also, we never were successful in finding a Golden-cheeked's nest, so we attempted to position ourselves close to one of the bird's singing perches as our most likely opportunity to score. We first listened for the song, which at times sounds remarkably like that of a Bewick's Wren, then clawed our way through the brush to where we thought the bird might be. This isn't difficult if you hear well and can directionally navigate the elusive,

Golden-cheeked Warbler, near Austin, Texas, 1991

Golden-cheeked Warbler, near Austin, Texas, 1993

ventriloquistic elements of this bird's song. I can't; Vera can, and time and again she saved the moment for us with this warbler. One morning, in fact, I ventured out by myself to find this bird, and indeed heard quite a few. However, I was not able to spot even one warbler, and spent the entire morning stumbling around the thick cedar brakes, lurching here and there, to absolutely no avail. The experience to this day remains one of Vera's favorite stories.

But finally we made it, just when we had all but concluded we might not. Our success did not occur, however, in April at the singing perches when males were establishing their territories, as we had imagined it would, but rather in June when the babies had just left the nest and were still being fed by the adults. One early June afternoon in a stand of old-growth cedars, we found the fledgling birds moving from tree to tree, limb to limb, closely attended to by both the male and female adults. We positioned ourselves as close to one of the fledglings as we could possible get, and as the male flew in to feed it, we squeezed off some shots that would be the first, and ultimately some of the best, we would get of this uncommon warbler.

And every spring thereafter, during the last weekend of March, we would make an obligatory pilgrimage to the Balcones Escarpment— to wade through the fresh bluebonnets of the surrounding meadows, inhale the aroma of Hill Country cedars after early morning rains, and pay our personal respects to the Golden-cheeked Warbler.

Fallout—High Island

EVEN though we had taken photographs of four warblers by the year 1990, these only represented the result of a growing general interest in wildlife photography itself. But 1990 was the year all that changed, the year we first challenged ourselves: "Wouldn't it be fun to see how many of these warblers we can photograph?" And it all started, appropriately enough, with a fallout at High Island.

At this very same place nearly eight years earlier, Vera had seen her first warblers, an event that would reawaken her interest in nature and wildlife and would launch her on a course to pursue her own definition of enchantment in the woods and fields and creek bottoms for years to come. It had been several years since we had experienced a fallout, and even though a rain-driven front had swept the Texas coast with heavy north winds the night before, we approached that next morning in late April 1990 with no particular expectation that this day would be significantly different from others of the recent past. But it was.

The morning was quiet, not much activity at all, and we spent our time covering Smith Woods at High Island with Jim Peterson, who had arrived just that morning after an all night drive from Dallas. At just about noon, we had called to Jim that we were going in for some lunch, when some movement caught our attention directly above us. Right there, on a drooping small oak branch not 15 feet from where we were standing, was a small bird, tired and barely moving as it slowly probed for insects. We instantly identified it as a Bay-breasted Warbler (no. 5), and we were able to get a respectable picture of it as it went about its business of devouring a large moth. We had never seen a Bay-breasted before, and although we would see many more that day and the next and on other occasions for several years to come, we would nevertheless

Bay-breasted Warbler (5), High Island, Texas, 1990

take this first photograph of this first fallout bird all the way with us to book form.

We were now no longer concerned with lunch that day as the trees, ground cover, and bushes began to fill up with tanagers, buntings, flycatchers, and of course, lots of warblers. We were able to get surprisingly near many of these birds, sometimes as close as 10–15 feet, and we were successful in getting flattering records of five brand-new warblers. In addition to the Bay-breasted, we also captured the Chestnut-sided (no. 6), the Black-throated Green (no. 7), the Magnolia (no. 8), and finally one of the most magnificent of them all, the Blackburnian (no. 9). The success we had during this weekend fallout at High Island confirmed for us that as improbable as it may have originally seemed, we could in fact get close enough to warblers, at least to some of them sometimes, to get respectable photographs. We were so encouraged by this prospect that a mildly aspirational next step was taken—to see how many of them we could actually get. It would be many birds later, however, as many as 30 or so down the road, that the final gear would engage—the commitment to try to photograph them all.

For the present, however, we were content with our first little victory of adding these five handsome, northern warblers to our modest list of four Texas birds. Bird no. 5 had been the Bay-breasted, a chocolate brown warbler that had always intrigued us even though we had never seen one before. This particular bird is a bit larger than most warblers and is more ponderously deliberate in its habits. It breeds in the northern United States and well into southern Canada and, like the Cape May, tends to annually relocate its nesting territory to follow recent outbreaks of spruce budworm. Uniquely, the female has been known to

Bay-breasted Warbler, Matagorda Island, Texas, 1992

Chestnut-sided Warbler (6), High Island, Texas, 1990

Chestnut-sided Warbler, New Preston, Connecticut, 1993

Black-throated Green Warbler (7), High Island, Texas, 1990

sing from her nest, although Vera and I were not in a position to validate this since we never found a nest of this bird. Didn't even look.

The Chestnut-sided Warbler (no. 6) always seemed to us to have a rather curious personality, and was easy to approach as we found it time and again nesting and feeding low in secondary growth and forest edges where heavy woods had been cleared. Many believe there are far more Chestnut-sideds today than there were two centuries ago, and it is said that James Audubon himself saw only one or two of these colorful warblers during his lifetime.

Warbler no. 7, the Black-throated Green, is a bird of the high conifers and mixed forests of the North. It is extremely plentiful in a range that has extended down through the Smokies and into the Ozarks of Arkansas. Vera and I found this bird from Manitoba to West Virginia to Grandfather's Mountain in North Carolina, but we never got closer to this bird than we did this day at High Island, or a couple of years later, also during migration, at Matagorda Island. The bird looks a great deal like a Golden-cheeked Warbler and is from the same ancient genetic stock that also produced the Hermit, the Black-throated Gray, and the Townsend's.

Bird no. 8, the Magnolia, is a special warbler to me, not only because it is remarkably handsome, but also because it was the first warbler I ever saw. This maiden sighting was in 1978 in New York City's Central Park, which interestingly enough is one of the best birding spots in the entire eastern United States during the first two weeks of May. Migratory songbirds winging north to New England and Canada find shelter and nourishment in this urban oasis rooted in the shadows of Manhattan skyscrapers. Hard-core birders take trains, or come by car, from distant suburbs in Connecticut and New Jersey into the bowels of Manhattan and then into the Park itself to experience this curious version of spring-migration birding.

As to my own knowledge of the subject at the time, "warbler" was only a vague word to designate some obscure bird that presumably "warbled," but that's about as far as it went. However, one early May

Magnolia Warbler (8), *High Island, Texas, 1990*

morning in 1978, when I was living in New York, my five-year-old son Mark and I were exploring the woody Ramble area of Central Park when we saw an elderly lady in sensible shoes and with binoculars looking at something high up in a large willow oak. We curiously and respectfully asked her what she was observing, and when she responded with, "Magnolia Warbler," nothing flashed at all. Nothing. She was nice enough, though, to let Mark and me take a look, and a whole new

Magnolia Warbler, Crane Creek, Ohio, 1992

world opened up. That the bird was exceptionally beautiful was impressive, to be sure, but I remember at the time being far more moved, and actually unsettled, by the realization that there was this colorful, new creature right "under my nose" that I had neither seen, nor even heard of before. It also substantiated the fact that people who aren't birders simply don't see what birders see and easily dismiss the activity as eccentric behavior, something decidedly light and trivial. When I was growing up in Texas, birdwatchers were considered to be quirky, certainly past middle age, and likely inclined to church socials and such. Real men hunted and fished, and young boys were raised to shoot birds, not to observe them. During those years, the rite of passage mandated shotguns for Christmas, not binoculars, and it's the binoculars that make the real difference—they're the key to the secret garden. They telescope size, magnify and intensify color, and allow a close observation of behavior, which in turn permits a special intimacy with the subject. Those without them are only faintly aware of some ill-defined, perhaps colorless object, flitting high left and off the radar. So Mark and I immediately rushed home to get binoculars and a bird book, and a totally new interest was born. It was the Magnolia Warbler that got it all started, a bird that understandably remains a favorite of mine today.

This warbler, a handsome black and yellow bird of the northern spruce and fir forests, is attractive in both attitude and behavior. It feeds low within its habitat, is easy to see, and relatively easy to approach, especially during migration. The bird winters in Central America and was perhaps on its way to Maine or even Canada when we were fortunate enough to intercept it at High Island. These were our first photographs of the Magnolia, but we ran across it often thereafter on its nesting grounds as well as on the Texas coast.

The last of the five birds we photographed that day, warbler no. 9, is considered by many to be even more striking than the Magnolia, and a bird that has seduced many a neophyte into the feverish advocacy of serious birding—namely, the Blackburnian Warbler. A high-treetop songbird of the north woods, it was called by the old-timers a "hemlock warbler," and its bright orange breast shining in the spring-morning sun is still considered one of the special thrills of North American birding. Blackburnians, however, are hard to approach on their nesting grounds. They tend to feed high in the trees, and their nests are also almost impossible to find at heights up to 100 feet. Consequently, the great "nest" photographers like Hal Harrison, Eliot Porter, and the Cottrilles had trouble with this bird. Catching them on migration, however, tired after a night flight over the Gulf of Mexico to the Texas coast, or over Lake Erie into Point Pelee, is a far more manageable exercise, and we picked up some reasonable shots of this fine bird that way. We also regularly encountered Blackburnians on their wintering grounds in the tropics. We fondly remember one foggy February morning in the Coastal Cordillera of northern Venezuela

OPPOSITE PAGE:
Blackburnian Warbler (9), *High Island, Texas, 1990*

Blackburnian Warbler, Sabine Woods, Texas, 1992

observing two brightly colored Blackburnian males feeding at eye level from the balcony of the old Rancho Grande Research Station in the Henri Pittier National Forest. Theoretically, Vera and I could have later encountered these same two "Venezuelan" birds on the Texas coast in late April, on the shores of Lake Erie in mid-May, and finally on one of their nesting grounds in Manitoba in early June.

After consolidating the successes we had during this late-April, High Island weekend, we decided to try for more warblers in East Texas. As we would so often do during those early years, we turned to Jim Peterson for advice as to our next step. He suggested we contact Dave Brotherton in Longview, who had spent a great deal of time working the area and knew its resident nesting species well. Consequently, a couple of weekends later we met Dave in the little town of Lone Star, Texas; and only a couple of miles away in some wild plum thickets, we jumped a colony of Prairie Warblers (no. 10). These were the first Prairie Warblers Vera and I had ever seen, and they proved to be responsive enough to tape recordings that we were able to coax one or two in for a close shot.

The Prairie Warbler is a bird that prefers overgrown thickets, abandoned pastures, and scrub pine plantations; and in future seasons, we would find them in this kind of habitat all through East Texas. More times than not, we would also encounter the Prairie's apparent running mate, the Yellow-breasted Chat, which seemed to prefer the same kind of neighborhood. However, Prairie colonies appeared to move around a lot, and we could never be sure from season to season that we would find them exactly where we had the year before.

This warbler is active and lively with a habit of bobbing its tail up and down, and also from side to side, like a Kirtland's or Palm Warbler. The female of the species has supposedly been known to sing herself, although we never had this validated for us. The most interesting thing

Blackburnian Warbler, Coastal Cordillera, Venezuela, 1992

Prairie Warbler (10), near Lone Star, Texas, 1990

Black-and-white Warbler (11), Caddo Lake, Texas, 1990

about the way this handsome bird looked, however, was not just the distinct black streaking on its forehead and the side of its face, but rather the chestnut streaking on its back, which, up close, looked like evenly spaced claw marks. A close-up photograph shows these markings, and we were able to get a few that first day, wading through the wild-plum meadows near Lone Star.

Not far from Lone Star is Caddo Lake, and the next weekend we went back there with no specific target in mind, except to finish up the season with anything we could run down. We were fortunate to maneuver close to a feeding Black-and-white Warbler (no. 11) that was working the bark of an ancient live oak so intently we were able to fire off a couple of shots of him before he even knew we were there. This marvelously patterned bird with its distinct black and white stripes and streaks is admired by most who encounter it, not only because of its striking appearance but also because of its somewhat peculiar feeding movements and style. It operates more times than not near eye level, as

Black-and-white Warbler, Caddo Lake, Texas, 1992

opposed to tree-top height, and is not dissimilar in behavior from the families of nuthatches that work tree barks in much the same way. Indeed, because the Black-and-white is more of a bark-probing specialist than other warblers dependent on spring-foliage insects, it is one of the early spring migrants to hit the Texas coast. It crosses the Gulf toward the end of March and then heads north before the rest of the country even begins to bloom. Although this is an easy bird to approach, it is nevertheless a very difficult bird to photograph as it is always moving—up a trunk, over a branch, down a limb, and maddeningly twitching its whole body from side to side like some wind-up toy as it quickly and deliberately covers its route. It was a difficult bird for us to get into tight focus, and through the years several ounces of soft, fuzzy slides of this sprightly little warbler found their way to the trash can. The Black-and-white was the last of the warblers we photographed in 1990. This gave us just 11, but we were nevertheless looking forward to the next year for which we had already set an interesting and ambitious agenda.

Matagorda Magic

THE first stop of our 1991 season was in mid-April at Matagorda Island, one of the five large barrier islands off the Gulf Coast of Texas. Matagorda is located about 125 miles southwest of Houston, and is separated by Cedar Bayou from another barrier island called St. Joseph's, owned by the Perry Bass family from Ft. Worth. Matagorda is an island with a colorful and rich history, and was Karankawa Indian territory until their ultimate demise in the 1850s in an extinction just as complete as that of the Passenger Pigeon, Carolina Parakeet, and Ivory-billed Woodpecker not that many years thereafter. Matagorda was also a running ground for such pirates as Jean Laffite. After the Civil War ranching activities dominated through the late 1800s and early 1900s. In the 1930s, the legendary oilman Clint Murchison assembled 11,500 acres on the south end of the island and built a large home on it for a retreat and requisite entertaining. When the partnership between Murchison and his lawyer, Toddie Wynne Sr., dissolved in 1946, Wynne wound up with Murchison's holdings on Matagorda. The compound would thereafter be known as Wynne Lodge, and a serious ranching enterprise was launched. The island resumed a colorful history through the ensuing years as such dignitaries as President Franklin Roosevelt, Arthur Godfrey, and the Duke and Duchess of Windsor found their way to Wynne Lodge. Also in 1981, the colorful Wynne, in what some local wags dismissed as a glorious but doomed crusade, promoted a private initiative to launch a commercial satellite into space from Matagorda. It blew up on the pad; but less than a year later, undeterred, Wynne initiated a second launch from Matagorda that proved successful.

In late 1986, the Nature Conservancy of Texas bought the Wynne holdings and combined this critical habitat with the existing Aransas Wildlife Refuge run by the U.S. Fish and Wildlife Service. For several

Hooded Warbler, Matagorda Island, Texas, 1991

years thereafter the Conservancy managed Wynne Lodge and its grounds as an environmental education center. I had joined the board of the Conservancy about this time, and Vera and I went down a couple of weekends a year with various groups to drum up support for conservation initiatives across the state.

The beauty and value of Matagorda lie in its extraordinary wildlife. With a mild climate, fertile bayside ponds, and tidal flats teeming with crabs, small fish, and mollusks, Matagorda is an important migratory stopover and/or wintering home for a large number of North American shorebirds and waterfowl. There are skimmers and gulls and terns. All of the herons and bitterns are represented. Ibises, storks, and Roseate Spoonbills show up in impressive numbers, and at least 15 species of duck settle in for the season. Although sandhill cranes also use the island during the winter, the feature attraction of Matagorda from November until March is unquestionably the Whooping Crane. This magnificent bird stands five feet tall and has a wingspan of more

OPPOSITE PAGE:
Hooded Warbler (12), *Matagorda Island, Texas, 1991*

than seven feet. It came within a flash of extinction in the 1930s, as its population had dwindled to but a few breeding pair. The bird breeds in the wild exclusively in the Wood Buffalo National Park in the Northwest Territories of Canada, and then in the fall practically the entire population of 140 or so flies over 2,600 miles to Aransas for the winter. Matagorda, which sits just across the bay from the Aransas Wildlife Refuge, has upward of 30–35 of these great birds wintering there.

Also, in the spring the songbirds that have been wintering in Mexico and in Central and South America make their way back across the Gulf to the U.S. mainland en route to their springtime nesting destinations. Matagorda serves as a brief stopover for a few strays that find temporary relief in the salt cedars that serve as a windbreak to the Wynne Lodge yard, and in some small live oaks back of the house. It was here in April 1991 that Vera and I picked up a few warblers that we had not yet photographed. It was also here that we tasted rattlesnake for the first time. One had crawled through a tear in the mesh fence that encloses the main lodge and was summarily dispatched as it was trying to crawl under the house. (All natural things on Matagorda are protected since it is a wildlife sanctuary, with the lone exception of poisonous snakes that get within the protected compound area.) Having heard that rattlesnake tasted very much like chicken, and since none of us had ever tried it before, we enthusiastically coaxed the cook into preparing it, which she reluctantly and sourly agreed to do. Then, under the breathless attention of the onlooking kitchen staff, we ate it. In fairness, it did taste something like chicken, but only marginally so, and it did not taste good. Even though we all put on our "game faces," and were trying desperately to be good sports, you could sense the unspoken resolve that this would likely be the last snake any of us would ever eat.

As to the warblers, the tamest of those we got close to that weekend was the Hooded Warbler (no. 12). It had blown in the same Friday night we arrived, and as I drifted out back the next morning with a cup of coffee in my hand, there it was—confidently bouncing along the back steps stalking insects for its own breakfast. I put down my coffee, retrieved my camera, and over the course of the next day or so, Vera and I snapped over a roll of pictures of this bird. It was no more complicated than that. The Hooded Warbler, with its unique "hangman" appearance, is a rather commonly found skulker of the dark swamp and bottomlands of the South and Midwest. Its song also has a robust musical quality to it, not unlike that of the Magnolia Warbler. Although this bird feeds and nests low to the ground, its behavior

Kentucky Warbler (13), *Matagorda Island, Texas, 1991*

reminds one of a flycatcher, as it fans its tail continuously while at the same time acrobatically swooping from low perches after insects. In fact, like all flycatchers, as well as the Canada Warbler, the Wilson's Warbler, and the redstarts, this bird has "whiskers" called rictal bristles for sensing and feeling insects as it tries to capture them during flight.

A neighbor of the Hooded Warbler, from a territory that is almost identical and in habitat roughly the same, is a black-sideburned denizen of the wooded understory, the Kentucky Warbler (no. 13). Through the years we would find this bird all the way from East Texas to East Tennessee, and almost always we would hear his loud and persistent song long before we were actually on him. The song itself resembles that of a Carolina Wren, and we were often fooled as to which one we were actually hearing. But this weekend we saw him first, and much like the Hooded, he was spending some time around the house in the shade

Yellow Warbler (14), *Matagorda Island, Texas, 1991*

looking for insects. However, we could not get near him at all as he was much jumpier than the Hooded, and at the first sign of approaching movement, he was gone. We did notice, however, that part of his routine around the lodge included some time on the roof, exploring for prey topside; so we simply worked a ladder up to the roof and,

Common Yellowthroat (15), *Matagorda Island, Texas, 1991*

partially shielded by a live oak we were standing next to, ambushed him when his feeding forays veered our way and also when he would drop from the roof to the ground below.

Some 30 minutes later, in a field nearby, fluttered in a Yellow Warbler (no. 14). We were then able to get our first picture of this bird, found in practically every state in the country, and known by many simply as a "wild canary." The bird is pretty and conspicuous and abundant; it prefers bright fields and yards, as opposed to dark ravines and bottoms, and chances are good that if one has seen but a single warbler, the Yellow Warbler would likely be that one. As the most widespread of all the warblers, we would later find it all the way from the cottonwood and willow trees of several western rivers to the wild rose tangles of Connecticut to the open meadows of southern Manitoba. Of all of the wood warblers of North America, the Yellow Warbler is clearly one of the best known.

Out back of Wynne Lodge is a perimeter fence, and lining this fence is the windbreak of salt cedars that serves as marvelous cover for migratory songbirds on their way north to the mainland. In this particular little stand of salt cedars, Vera and I would, over the next three or four years, encounter many a warbler during migration; but the first we were to come across this same weekend was another very common and sprightly undergrowth mover known as the Common Yellowthroat (no. 15). It was searching for insects and grubs at the base of these dense trees, which were so thick and close to the ground that it was hard to even see the bird, much less get a clear shot of it. It nevertheless moved in a rather predictable and oft-repeated pattern from west to east along the fence line, and we were able to take a picture from time to time as it bounced through an open area between two sections of dense shrub near a small pond. Known as the "little masked bandit" because of its unusual facial markings, it is often found in marshy habitat around streams and ponds. Its song is loud, with a distinctive rhythm, and is usually launched from a favorite perch. We would see and hear this ubiquitous bird many times, and in a variety of different habitats, as we crossed the country trying to locate and photograph all of the warblers.

Common Yellowthroat, Dallas, Texas, 1996

The Chiricahuas

THE end of April presented us with an opportunity to visit the East Coast, as business pulled me to New York, and Vera and I were able to stay over the weekend in New England to run down some of the warblers of that area. One locale reputed to be good for migratory songbirds was hinged in the northwest quadrant of Connecticut, outside of the quaint little community of Kent. Crossing the Housatonic River traveling west through town and veering right as you approach the Kent School, you come to a road that soon turns into a small dirt path that parallels the river. This little stretch is aptly known as "River Road," and here, each spring, birders flock to catch migratory waves of songbirds drifting north along this particular band of flyway. For reasons that were not clear, we had that entire Saturday morning, flush in the heart of the high season, all to ourselves. The only people we saw were a small group of four coming down the road as we were leaving about noon. They were anxious and excited to find the Yellow-throated Warbler, which had presumably been spotted in the area the day before, a springtime rarity for this part of New England, to be sure, but extremely common in East Texas and not the object of our own search that day. This morning for us was notable for the one bird we actually did photograph, the Golden-winged Warbler (no. 16), and for one that we almost captured, a Cerulean Warbler. The latter picture, however, was just a bit soft, rendering it unacceptable, but it could have been a great one because the Cerulean is a beautiful bird to begin with, and this specimen was feeding in a flowering cherry tree. A cerulean blue bird against a rose pink background is about as good as a photograph setting gets, but it was simply not to be; and the Cerulean, unfortunately without the cherry tree, would have to await another day.

Golden-winged Warbler (16), *Kent, Connecticut, 1991*

As for the Golden-winged, we were extremely fortunate, because in a back meadow about 150 yards from the road we first heard, then saw this magnificent and handsomely patterned warbler. It responded to a tape recording just one time for a total of about 20 seconds, but that was just long enough for us to fire off a couple of shots of it. We would find this bird with some predictability from West Virginia to Michigan, but in this case, the first encounter seemed to be the best, and we would remember our morning on the River Road for some time to come. Several years later, however, we managed another acceptable picture of this bird under the direction of that knowledgeable East Tennessee birder Fred Alsop, when we jumped several males in a high meadow at Hampton Creek Cove, Tennessee.

The Golden-winged is in many respects an exceptional bird, not only because of its elegantly handsome appearance and buzzy, insect-like song, but because it sometimes hybridizes with the Blue-winged Warbler. The two are known to interbreed in the overgrown meadows, weedy pastures, and secondary-growth areas in the central part of eastern North America where their two ranges overlap. The initial pairing produces the hybrid form known as the Brewster's Warbler, which usually carries the coloration of a white throat and underparts, with some yellow wash on the breast. The much rarer Lawrence's Warbler is the recessive byproduct of a Brewster's pairing with either a Blue-winged or a Golden-winged, themselves carrying recessive genes from a

Golden-winged Warbler, Hampton Creek Cove, Tennessee, 1998

previous cross, and is distinguished in its own coloration by a black throat and mask on a predominantly yellow body. The only time I ever saw a Lawrence's was very early in this birding effort when my daughter Laura and I had a fleeting glance of one about 90 feet up in a laurel oak tree in Central Park. I did not see it all that well, and was much too inexperienced to have appreciated its significance even if I had. Nevertheless, there was a feverish knot of birders huddled around the tree screaming, "Lawrence's, Lawrence's," much as if there had been some Elvis sighting, so even I knew that something momentous had occurred. As for the Brewster's, Vera and I have seen it twice—once in East Texas on migration and the other time on its nesting grounds in East Tennessee. On this latter occasion, we actually got a picture of it, but it was only one shot, a C+ record at best. Even though the Blue-winged and Golden-winged have significantly overlapping ranges that permit this hybridizing, the Blue-winged tolerates a wider band of habitat than does the Golden-winged, and is rapidly replacing it in their common ranges.

A couple of thousand miles west of the Housatonic was a completely different warbler range, and Vera and I headed there next to seek out a group of western warblers that we had never even seen before, much less photographed. The spot was Cave Creek, Arizona, and it is one of the most popular birdwatching locales in all of North America—with good reason. The diversity of the wildlife at Cave Creek has everything to do with its topography: a mountain range called the Chiricahuas explodes suddenly from the desert floor to 10,000 feet, creating five different life zones—from Sonoran to Canadian—and converging both northern and southern species of birds into one spot. Because of this diversity of habitat, the area has an extraordinarily impressive variety of breeding land birds, and the latest count puts the number at 190. Here colored cliffs frame valleys and creek beds of oak, juniper, and sycamore; and a land once noted for Cochise and Geronimo now boasts 15 different species of hummingbirds, 12 varieties of owls, and that special rarity from Mexico, the Elegant Trogon. Plus, of course, warblers—eight different species of them. We were to come away from this first trip to Arizona with photographs of only three of these birds, although we were able to find and briefly observe all eight.

It began the first day we were there. In late afternoon, we were walking almost aimlessly down the oak- and juniper-lined South Fork Road leading to Cave Creek when a small, gray, white, and black bird began slowly and deliberately feeding in a short juniper close to where

Black-throated Gray Warbler (17), *Cave Creek, Arizona, 1991*

we were standing. For a moment we thought it was a chickadee, but on closer inspection, it became clear it was a Black-throated Gray Warbler (no. 17), with its telltale yellow-orange dot right in front of the eye. This attractive bird of the juniper and oak forests of New Mexico, Arizona, and Colorado has color patterns almost identical to that of the Townsend's Warbler, except that where the Black-throated Gray has white, the Townsend's has yellow. The bird also seems fearless when it comes to humans, and we found it very easy to approach the few times we encountered this bird in Arizona and Colorado over the next several years.

The next morning, unencumbered by any pretense that we knew what we were doing in Arizona, we accepted the help of a local bird expert of the region, Bob Morse, who had agreed to guide us for our first morning here in the Chiricahuas. He took us first to Rustler Park, up the mountain out of the oak belt into the cool ponderosa pine,

Olive Warbler (18), Cave Creek, Arizona, 1991

Olive Warbler, Cave Creek, Arizona, 1991

aspen, and white fir groves some 8,500 feet above sea level. The initial place we stopped was near a fork in the road called Onion Saddle, and we walked back into the trees to where Bob thought we might find the Olive Warbler (no. 18). We did. No sooner had he given a couple of toots from a tape of the song of the Olive male than one appeared, no more than 12 feet away. It blew in so quickly, in a maneuver so swift and unforeseen, that Vera and I simply stood frozen, ill prepared to take any advantage of the opportunity. But fortunately, as the bird looked for small grubs that had been part of a recent outbreak in the area, we recovered and were able to net several good photographs of this uncommonly colored warbler. One of the reasons birders fancy this warbler so much is precisely its color, which is not an "olive" at all, but rather a tawny orange or persimmon that is distinctive among songbirds. Its deliberate behavior is also a bit unusual, more like that of a chickadee than the fluttering movements of most warblers. Additionally peculiar, its tail is notched in an odd way, and its eggs, unlike those of any other warbler, are darkly smudged. These differences, along with a variety of other taxonomic features, have led some ornithologists to suggest that perhaps the Olive Warbler is not really a warbler at all and should be summarily declassified and drummed out of the warbler corps. Those of us who don't care much about the technical elements of the issue, however parochial and cavalier that attitude may be, hope they fail. We like the Olive Warbler being a warbler; we feel it adds color to the whole family.

The afternoon of that same day, we drifted down the mountain and into the sycamore and oak trees of Cave Creek Canyon, arguably one of the most beautiful areas in Arizona. We had the entire creek bottom to ourselves, and we were hopeful that we might find the striking Elegant Trogon that had recently been seen in this area. We didn't, but what we did find was every bit as exciting—a pair of Painted Redstarts (no. 19). They were working low, feeding young way back in a nest so hidden that we never actually saw it. For the next hour or so we stood

Painted Redstart (19), *Cave Creek, Arizona, 1991*

Painted Redstart, Cave Creek, Arizona, 1991

frozen, except for the occasional photograph of the action, watching these magnificent birds come and go to the nest site with beaks full of insect food. It was the first time Vera and I had seen these colorful and acrobatic birds—brilliantly colored in red, white, and black, fluttering from tree to bush to nest, constantly fanning their tails like dancing butterflies. Most migrating warblers molt into colorful springtime plumage and then back again into their "confusing fall colors," and the coloration between male and female can be distinctly different especially in the spring. The male and female Painted Redstarts, however, look the same all year long. This is understandable since these particular birds are actually Mexican warblers that migrate to the northern edge of their range barely over the U.S. border and are part of the tropical family of warblers in which male and female have almost identical color patterns.

Wilson's Warbler (20), Vail, Colorado, 1991

On leaving Cave Creek and southern Arizona and before returning to Texas, we spent a few days in Vail, Colorado, visiting Vera's daughters, Rhonda and Cindy. Although we didn't have much free time to look for warblers, we were nevertheless able to spend one or two mornings out in the woods. One day we climbed a mountain just north of Vail to a beautiful valley surrounded by small ponds near Piney Ranch. In the thick grass and willows near one of these ponds we heard the song of a bird we could not identify, although it had a persistent staccato trill. The bird was so well hidden we could not see it, and circling maneuvers to get a clear look proved futile. The only thing we knew to do under these circumstances was to try to coax the bird out into the open, so we began "pishing." Immediately the bird responded, and we could tell by the way the brush was moving that it was slowly and deliberately inching our way. Within about 10 seconds, it stuck its head through the reeds to sneak a peek at us, and we in turn were able to get a good look at it—a small, yellow bird with the telltale black cap atop its head, the Wilson's Warbler (no. 20). The Wilson's is energetic and relatively curious, not only on its nesting ground but also in its wintering territories, and it was not at all unusual that we were able to lure it close enough to get a couple of photographs. We would see this nifty little bird many times thereafter on its wintering grounds in Houston and again in Saltillo, Mexico, but it was here in Vail where we saw it first, and our picture of it was the only one that proved acceptable for publication.

Little Sandy

As we returned to Texas in mid-June, we concluded that our 1991 season was just about over since most of the birds back home were in postnesting modes and thus would be more difficult to locate and approach. However, we were not home more than several days when we received a call from a friend in East Texas, Guy Luneau, who told us that he had located a singing Swainson's Warbler (no. 21) in a water elm thicket near the small town of Gilmer. Vera and I immediately headed that way, because we had never seen the Swainson's before, much less taken any photographs of it. It proved, however, far more difficult to locate that morning than we had presumed, and we floundered around in very thick undergrowth for quite some time before we finally heard the bird sing. But what a song it was—a series of loud, clear, and even-pitched whistles followed by a distinct and deliberate "warble." As we discovered over the years, most of the warblers we encountered couldn't carry a tune at all, and most of them, even on their best days in the spring of their very best years, sounded no better than loud insects. The song of the Swainson's, exceptional by comparison, is a complex and musical product that gives it distinction in the warbler world. It greatly impressed Vera and me at the time, and the song remains to this day our favorite. We were also fortunate enough to snap several pictures of the bird actually singing, our most unusual being a frontal shot showing its head pointed straight up toward the East Texas sky. The Swainson's, however, sings much better than it looks, as it is an unremarkably plain, buff and brown bird with a soft, brown crown and a long, pointed bill. It is a low understory resident of the southern canebrakes and bottomlands, and it is not all that common even in territories where it is known to nest. This Swainson's taken near Gilmer, Texas, was the only one Vera and I ever came across, either on its nesting grounds or on migration, and we remembered it fondly, less for the way it looked than for the wonderful song it made.

Gilmer is only about 35 minutes from our weekend home in East Texas at the Little Sandy Hunting and Fishing Club, which is itself only about one and a half hours due east of Dallas. The club was founded in 1907 and most of its 75 or so members regard it highly for the quality of its bass fishing and duck hunting. But its character has a lot more to do with the fact that its main lake has as its original core one of the few natural lakes in Texas, originally formed as an ancient oxbow of the Sabine River. Consequently the lake is home to some rather primitive species like the alligator snapping turtles, which are known to grow to 150 pounds and are occasionally shipped to zoos around the country. The lake also supports a large population of alligators, roosting egrets and herons, and a large variety of songbirds. Its reputation is not, however, based entirely on either its game management or its indigenous wildlife, but rather on its trees. The Little Sandy

Swainson's Warbler (21), near Gilmer, Texas, 1991

Swainson's Warbler, near Gilmer, Texas, 1991

tract of 3,500 acres is one of the largest virgin hardwood bottomlands left in the South, with trees that are several hundred years old. The club therefore brags less on its fishing and hunting than it does on the fact that over the years it has had trees on its property that have held both state and national records. In 1988, the Nature Conservancy of Texas helped the club structure a conservation easement on this acreage so that this national treasure could be protected forever.

Also on the club's property, in a grove of giant loblolly pines, is a small cottage that Vera and I use as a weekend home. Right outside this cottage, throughout the year, including the winter months, we can hear the song of the Pine Warbler high up in those pines. The Pine is a rather drab, washed-out yellow bird with a distinctive trill of a song, a lot like that of the Chipping Sparrow. It does not migrate very far south in the winter, usually no farther than the southern United States,

Pine Warbler (22), near Hawkins, Texas, 1991

and hence our opportunity to hear its song even on cold December days. But this Pine Warbler (no. 22) would be remembered to us, not because of how it looked or even sounded, but rather because of how it behaved one June morning when we played back the tape of its song. It first flew down to a lower branch to check us out. Nothing unusual there. Then, however, this bird began to drop ever so slowly in a floating, fluttering motion much like that of a falling leaf—all the way to the ground. It looked up at us for a few seconds, and then it flew to a short bush nearby while we fired two shots. Then it flew back up into the trees. We were stunned. We had never seen a bird do anything remotely close to that before. And we never would again. Vera, who possesses an impressive capacity for astonishment, felt a sudden urge to name this special bird. To me this warbler was just a plain little bird that had admittedly put on a remarkable performance, but to Vera it romantically became our "Fluttering Angel." And though that label was understandably too precious for me, it was nevertheless the one she always used when remembering our resident Pine Warbler of the loblolly pines at Little Sandy.

More Migratory Traps

AS 1991 came to a close, we took stock of what we had accomplished over the previous two years and concluded that, by and large, it hadn't been much. We had admittedly taken some reasonably good pictures of a total of 22 warblers, had seen some scenically diverse parts of the country, and had thoroughly enjoyed the process of the hunt and the enchantment of the quarry. But with perhaps the exception of the Swainson's, all 22 of these warblers were considered to be pretty easy birds to capture on film, and we knew that our biggest challenges lay ahead.

We decided that if this particular warbler quest was going to go anywhere at all, then 1992 was lining up to be a critical year for us. We would need to run down some of the really "tough ones," and then be successful in bagging decent photographs of them. Vera and I would begin our 1992 season quite naturally enough trying to intercept birds on migration in April and early May as they crossed some major body of water. This year, in addition to our usual spots on the Texas Gulf Coast, we decided to try a couple of new locales, equally famous as migratory traps—Point Pelee in Ontario, and the Dry Tortugas, some 70 miles off the Florida Keys.

Our first stop, however, was Sabine Woods. It was here in this woodlot over the last several years that we had been successful in finding good clusters of warblers that had just crossed the Gulf and "fallen" into this particular oak motte to rest and feed. We were here the third weekend in April, and although there had been a thunderstorm the night before, the wind had shifted to southerly and the prospects of having an extraordinary day were slim. Not unexpectedly, we spent the entire morning without success, despite encountering impressive populations of Indigo Buntings and Red-eyed Vireos. We were about to

Cape May Warbler (23), near Sabine Pass, Texas, 1992

Cape May Warbler, near Sabine Pass, Texas, 1992

Cape May Warbler, Comber, Ontario, 1992

break for lunch when we met up with Victor Emanuel, who was leading an eco-tour group to the Gulf Coast and who also looked upon Sabine Woods as a productive and, at times, more manageable alternative to the increasingly crowded High Island. We visited awhile, compared notes, and then Victor suggested that Vera and I try the salt cedars closer to the water, which lined the road in intermittent clumps all the way to Galveston and also the Sabine Pass jetty road jutting south. At our first stop we saw nothing, and while Vera was exploring the back of the original stand, I crossed the highway to check out clump number two. There I walked right up to an almost stationary Cape May Warbler (no. 23) in full breeding plumage. Vera came over and we both took several shots before this lovely bird disappeared back into the brush, but we came back the next day and were once again successful with it. Vera and I acknowledged that we owed this Cape May to Victor, since we would certainly not have thought to look in the salt cedars for it without his direction and encouragement.

The Cape May is clearly one of our most elegant warblers, with the tiger-streaked yellow breast and the telltale chestnut cheek patch. It is a bird of northern New England and Canada, having no relevant connection to its namesake Cape May, New Jersey, except that it was first discovered and named there as it traveled through on migration. This bird is not much of a singer, with but a weak and squeaky song, and it is extremely difficult to find with any consistency on its nesting grounds. The Cape Mays cannot be counted on to ever nest in the same locale twice, as their nesting sites are dependent on the most recent outbreak of its favorite food source, the spruce budworm. It therefore is inclined to go where the budworm goes. In high infestation years, the Cape May will opportunistically lay more eggs, and there are reports of occasional nests with eight to nine eggs in them. Another peculiarity of this bird is that it is equipped with a tubular-configured tongue that allows it to feed on the juice of berries, and not a few vineyards have had their grape harvests ravaged by migrating Cape Mays working their way south in the fall.

On Sunday of that same weekend, we were winding up our stay at Sabine Woods, with but the lone Cape May to our credit, when we heard some commotion on the west side of the woodlot, suggesting that someone had discovered a bird of real interest. They had—a Cerulean Warbler (no. 24), one of the prettiest and most coveted of all the wood warblers that nest in the United States. There was only one of them, a lone male, working the low, sweeping limbs of one of the

Cerulean Warbler (24), near Sabine Pass, Texas, 1992

Cerulean Warbler, Princeton, West Virginia, 1996

giant live oaks near the pond. We stationed ourselves behind some low brush directly in his feeding path, and we were able to get some fairly good shots, so intent was he on eating. Vera took one striking picture of the Cerulean crouching in a cherry laurel nearby, nanoseconds before it jumped a hapless insect.

The Cerulean is a creature of mature woodlands and river drainages dominated by large trees and is known to build its nest from 40 to 70 feet high. Since its song is an unremarkable, buzzy trill, and since most views of it are from below looking high up to its white breast and thin, identifying dark breast band, this bird would seem to have little to recommend it. But up close, its topside color is a blue so different from that of other blue birds that it is considered to be in a class all by itself. Some call it a heavenly blue or sweet-sky blue, and it is this color that captivates all birdwatchers and bird photographers alike. The most impressive photograph we ever saw of the Cerulean was a nest shot of

Cerulean Warbler, near Sabine Pass, Texas, 1992

a sitting female, attended to closely by the male, taken by Betty Cottrille. The color rendition was perfect and both birds were in tack-sharp focus. But what made the picture sensational was the location of the nest—40 feet high when the picture was taken. Betty and her husband, Powell, and Eliot Porter found it necessary to build a scaffold that high in order to position the camera and flash equipment at eye level for the pictures. Vera and I had it easy by comparison, and although we would take many photographs of this bird through the years, from Arkansas to Connecticut to West Virginia, we always felt these Sabine Woods shots were our most interesting. Unfortunately, populations of this splendid bird are diminishing rapidly—perhaps at a greater rate than any other warbler, due to the decline of our river bottomlands as well as the accelerating deforestation of the Ceruleans' winter home in the northern Andes. Our success here at Sabine, however, capped a terrific weekend and an encouraging start to our 1992 season, a start that included both the Cape May and the Cerulean—two of the best.

Our next stop was another migratory trap that we had heard a lot about and were eager to try: a chain of tropical islands 70 miles off Key West called the Dry Tortugas. The area is especially revered in world birding circles for its impressive colonies of Sooty Terns and Brown Noddies that nest there on Bush Key. Since Vera and I were not tern and noddie kind of people, our interest exclusively lay in the migrating songbirds passing over on their flight across the Gulf to reach the Florida mainland. To get there, we took an all-night boat ride out of Key West and arrived about dawn at historic Fort Jefferson, which anchors the Dry Tortugas. When the weather is just right, with winds and rain out of the north, the birding here from fallouts can be extraordinary. This time, however, winds blew steadily from the south, and while we saw a lot of birds, including a fair number of warblers and a rare Golden Eagle, we were not able to run down any of the warbler rarities that had been our original hope. Additionally, Vera became ill with high fever, most likely aggravated by dehydration, and we took a quick trip back to Key West midmorning by a seaplane that had been called over from the mainland to get us. This minicrisis came to a peaceful end, without entirely eliminating the unease it had created, and we could never thereafter get all that enthusiastic about going back to the Dry Tortugas for another attempt.

The best spot at Fort Jefferson to find birds is at the fountain in the center of the fort's courtyard, which has the only fresh water on the

American Redstart (25), *Dry Tortugas, 1992*

island. It consequently serves as a magnet for all migrating birds that need fresh water both for drinking and for washing the salt from their feathers. The fountain, however, also serves as a magnet for gaggles of flash photographers who stake out vantage points in large numbers and more than just a little detract from the charm of the wildlife experience. That little watering hole nonetheless is where the action takes place at Fort Jefferson, and if you want to get good photographs of songbirds there, you're obliged to put in your share of fountain time. We were, however, on a random sortie outside of the fort, several hours before Vera got sick, when we picked up our only keeper warbler of the trip, thus preventing a total bust. It was an American Redstart (no. 25), tired and low to the ground, and although this bird is commonly found throughout the eastern United States, practically everywhere warblers are found, we took our best photographs of it here on the Dry Tortugas. This flycatcher-type warbler, with its jet black body and patches of orange on its wings, is prone to acrobatic maneuvers as it sallies forth to snatch insect prey. With constant fluttering and pirouetting with its tail flashing and fanning, it resembles a small, ornamental oriole in motion.

MORE MIGRATORY TRAPS

After Sabine Woods and the Dry Tortugas, the next stop on our migratory-trap run was Lake Erie and the two famous collecting points and staging areas—Crane Creek and Point Pelee. Crane Creek and its Magee Marsh Wildlife Area is located due east of Toledo on the south side of Lake Erie, and during mid-May each year, the songbird population builds here to fuel up before making the flight across the lake to the southern shores of Ontario. If the wind has been blowing steadily out of the north for several days, the birds begin to stack up waiting for southerly breezes to kick in that will easily blow them across. Vera and I arrived amid just such conditions and were greeted by a profusion of songbirds, including more than 20 species of warblers. These were also fairly easy to see up close as we worked the boardwalk that snaked through the best of the habitat there. Although we encountered

Blackpoll Warbler (26), *Crane Creek, Ohio, 1992*

Blackpoll Warbler, Crane Creek, Ohio, 1992

and photographed many warblers during our two-day stay in the area, the most memorable and our best photograph was that of the Blackpoll (no. 26). The Blackpoll is a truly remarkable bird, not because of its coloration, which is similar to that of the Black-and-white, and not even because of its song, although its register is the highest of any warbler. No, this warbler is unique because of its migratory prowess. In the fall of each year, this ½-ounce, 5 ½-inch bird of the northern spruce forests will drift easterly to Nova Scotia and New England, where for several days it will double its fat reserves in preparation for the migratory return to its tropical winter home. Nothing unusual there. The trip south, however, is—a nonstop journey of more than three days and 2,500 miles out over the Atlantic all the way from Nova Scotia to Venezuela or Brazil for the season! Almost unbelievable! Although many of the songbirds travel great distances, and many also cross imposing expanses of water, the Blackpoll outranks all other warblers in this event, and is nearly on a par with the Arctic Tern and the Golden Plover for long-distance-travel honors. Our experience with it, however, was not particularly noteworthy as we spotted it late on the afternoon of the second day in a willow tree very near the boardwalk where we were prowling. We nonchalantly walked up to it and took several pictures. As simple as that. We had wished they were all that way.

The night of that same day, the winds shifted and began to blow out of the south. Consequently, we knew it was time to move on, and we drove through the night up to Detroit and then eastward to Leamington, Ontario, which would position us on the northern shore of the same body of water that the birds we had seen for several days at Crane Creek would now be crossing. We dragged in late that night to a bed-and-breakfast called Home Suite Home, run by a charming and colorful couple, Aggie and Harry Tiesson. We then prepared ourselves for an early-morning ambush of the night-flying warblers now crossing

Palm Warbler (27), *Point Pelee, Ontario, 1992*

Palm Warbler, Point Pelee, Ontario, 1992

Lake Erie and heading for that famous peninsula where they would likely touch down—Point Pelee.

Point Pelee National Park is legendary as a remarkable migratory concentration point. It juts southward nine miles out into Lake Erie, thereby serving as a funnel for the birds crossing the lake. The tip of the point is the first land the night-flying birds see, and during mid-May each year they come down here to rest and feed. Upward of 300 different species of birds have been recorded at Point Pelee, including 30 different kinds of warblers and, as one might also expect, lots of people. It was therefore crowded the next morning with birders who themselves had funneled into the Point overnight for their annual rendezvous with the birds.

There was a great deal of activity that day, and we were able to see many birds, including a number of warblers. Yet while we spent the whole day on our feet walking up and down the Point, we were unable to get close enough to any one bird for a decent shot. Late that afternoon, however, on the western shore of the Point, we encountered a cruising colony of Palm Warblers (no. 27) feeding in some high grass and were able to capture a few pictures of which we were proud. The Palm is a tail-bobbing bird that nests in the spruce bogs of the North, and winters in the Bahamas and Antilles, although many simply stay over in Florida for the season. It is, in fact, extremely common to find large and easily observable populations of Palm Warblers in Florida all winter long. Despite our day's slow start, we were able to end on a high note with this handsome bird taken late in the afternoon.

The next morning was pretty much the same as the day before. We saw lots of warblers, but they were all flitting too high in the trees for us to get close enough to do any good. We broke for lunch, tired and frustrated with the anxiety of a marvelous opportunity slipping away, as we had very little to show for our efforts to date and were scheduled to leave the next day. Then a peculiar thing happened. Over lunch in a small diner at the edge of the park, we overheard a birding group gushing over some success they had that morning at an obscure spot some 15 miles or so north of Leamington called Comber. Feeling we had nothing much to lose at this point, we abandoned Point Pelee and headed north toward Comber in search of whatever action we could stumble across. We found Comber easily enough but concluded that our inspired little plan had failed in execution because this little rural community had all the unpretentious charm and promise of a pit stop in the middle of an Iowa cornfield. Here in this truck-farming area of Ontario, far from any apparent water or trees or decent habitat, it sat. We were more or less ready to turn back when down a side road about 200 yards away we spotted a small willow and hardwood marsh area that, as we were soon to discover, was covered up with birds. And with lots of warblers! This one little spot of decent habitat was an oasis in the middle of nowhere. Nowhere, that is, except directly in the path of thousands of migrating songbirds funneling up from Point Pelee on their northward course toward the Canadian woods.

We saw Parulas, a female Kentucky, scores of Cape Mays, Magnolias, Prothonotaries, Palms, and many more. This was a warbler "honey hole," and we spent the entire afternoon there taking pictures of the birds. One in particular we photographed that day was the Myrtle Warbler (no. 28), which is the eastern variety of the ubiquitous Yellow-rumped Warbler. The most numerous of all the warblers by several orders of magnitude, the Myrtle in the East and its equivalent, the

Myrtle Warbler (28), Comber, Ontario, 1992

Audubon's in the West, were considered to be two separate species until the early 1970s. But ornithologists found that where the range of the two birds overlapped, they were prone to interbreed. Hence the combination of the two species into one, renamed the Yellow-rumped for its most common and distinctive feature. Both the Myrtle and the Audubon's have this yellow rump in addition to a distinctive yellow patch on their crown. But where the Myrtle has a black face mask, the Audubon's has a black eyeline; and where the Myrtle has a white throat, the Audubon's has a yellow one. What makes the Yellow-rumped distinctive, with both its Audubon's and Myrtle variations, is the huge geographical area over which it ranges, and consequently the wide diversity of habitats it will accept. Yellow-rumpeds are found everywhere from coastal pines to just below the timberline to dense spruce and fir forests to scruffy edge clearings. Like all warblers, it is insectivorous, but this bird has far more variety in its diet than most, with a particular fondness for the berries of many shrubs, including those of the myrtle family in particular. Because of this feeding behavior, which permits the digestion of the waxy coating of berries, the Yellow-rumped doesn't feel the compulsion to flee far south when winds begin to turn out of the north in autumn. Some Myrtles actually stay to winter in the United States, a few as far north as New England in some years, while most other species of warblers drift back south to the tropics for the season. The only time Vera and I would see these birds in Texas would indeed be during the winter, when they would be around in great numbers, but not in the breeding plumage necessary for flattering photographs. Consequently, we had to migrate north ourselves in May to the unlikely community of Comber, Ontario, to get a respectable photograph of this Myrtle version of the Yellow-rumped.

Connecticut Warbler (29), near Solon Springs, Wisconsin, 1992

Of Kirtland's and Cowbirds

AFTER Point Pelee we wanted to pursue the Kirtland's Warbler. Our schedule dictated, however, that we first tackle another warbler that was known to be uncommon on its territory, with a nest almost impossible to find, one seldom even seen on migration—the Connecticut Warbler (no. 29). Its scarcity was attested to by the fact that through the years we had seen only two or three decent photographs of it at all. We had heard that some Connecticuts had been taken in the spruce bogs of Minnesota up near Ely, so we set sail for Duluth in the hopes of locating this extremely elusive and secretive bird. We knew that if we had any pretensions at all of ever finding most of the warblers, that the first real test we faced would be the Connecticut. Pretty pictures of Magnolias and Chestnut-sideds were fine and good, but we would have to begin tackling the tough targets on this trip, and tough-target number one was this bird. We did some preparation before hitting Minnesota and lined up Kim Eckert, a tour leader for Victor Emanuel, to be our guide. Kim lived in Duluth, and we started early the next morning to explore some of the general area for a few other warblers we needed before concentrating on the real focus of our visit to Minnesota. We encountered Black-throated Blues, Canadas, and even one brilliant Blackburnian, but our photographic opportunities were mediocre at best, and both Vera and I were becoming anxious to get on with the main event.

And so early the next morning, flush with the fragrance of a lime green spring and buoyed with high hopes, we began—not up toward the spruce bogs near Ely where we had convinced ourselves most Connecticut Warblers lived, but south into northern Wisconsin and the jack pines northeast of Solon Springs where Kim Eckert knew some did. South of Superior, out of Lake Nebagamon, a dirt road S crosses the

Brule River and runs through the sandy jack pine country. There we found the Connecticut Warbler, just as Kim knew we would—at least two of them that first morning. The birds looked very much like the Mourning Warbler and the MacGillivray's Warbler, both cousins of the Connecticut. The Connecticut, however, has a full and clearly distinct white eye ring, while the other two do not, and this is the best way to mark their differences. We spent most of the afternoon trying to get close to one of their singing perches for at least a picture of record, but to little avail. We even tried to bring them in by tape, but they simply flew over us from one tall tree to the other in order to get a better view of the singing intruder. We did manage to get off one shot at about 45 feet, but we regrettably felt certain that it would not be of respectable quality.

The next morning we went back to the same spot, this time without Kim, for he had already done his part by putting us squarely on the birds in the first place. We drilled far deeper into the woods and jumped three additional singing male Connecticuts. Our results were at first pretty much the same, with the warblers acknowledging the sound coming from the tape recording but guardedly keeping their distance from both it and us. But finally the fourth bird of the day acted differently. In fact, it behaved a lot differently in that it blew right into the sound of the tape not 15 feet from where we were standing. Vera and I were able to get some adequate shots before the bird flew down from the branch where it had been observing us onto the ground. Then, in a manner that we will never forget, it slowly began to walk—not hop, but walk—through the dense understory in a circling maneuver to sneakily approach us from the other side. Vera and I stood motionless, and every now and then we could pinpoint where the little guy was located by the barely perceptible movement of some brush or understory grass. It finally showed itself again, and we were able to take a few more rushed shots before it finally flew off. We felt we had been gifted with a splendid opportunity with this bird, and we were confident that at least one of our photographs would turn out. So we enthusiastically declared victory and, at least for that evening, congratulated ourselves on having captured one of the very toughest of all the warblers. We also allowed ourselves to muse that perhaps, just perhaps, we might now have a real shot at photographing all of these birds. It was on this very evening, buoyed by our Connecticut Warbler success, yet strangely with no wine involved, that we moved our project decisively forward—from photographing a lot of warblers, to trying to photograph them all. There was, as we would find out over the following several years, a substantial difference between the two.

We left Wisconsin late that afternoon and drove across the Upper Peninsula of Michigan until we reached the little community of Grand Marais, snug on Lake Superior. Powell and Betty Cottrille had their summer home there, and Powell had encouraged us to try this area for our photography. He felt it was the most prolific place he knew for wood warblers, to which he passionately and often referred as his "jewels of the woods." The countryside was beautiful, and we were particularly impressed by the spruce bogs there that the Cottrilles memorialized, almost reverently, as their "cathedrals." After several days in the region and with some small measure of success, Vera and I needed a break from this bird business, so we dropped down into the Lower Peninsula for some R and R in the lovely little resort community of Harbor Springs, Michigan, where we ate well and slept late for a couple of days.

By the first part of the following week it was time to rev up again and take a stab at another one of our big challenges—the Kirtland's Warbler (no. 30). We moved on to the one area of the world where you can find this bird, a 6,000-acre tract of jack pines near Mio, Michigan. We knew we wouldn't have any trouble finding the Kirtland's, as there were guided tours through this warbler's habitat each day. What we did worry about, and with good reason, was getting close enough to the bird to get its picture, since we knew that once we committed ourselves to the tour, we would be confined inflexibly to the marked paths through its official territory. Also, since this bird was labeled an endangered species, tape-playing was out of the question. We had already resigned ourselves to the tour program when, in a good-bye telephone conversation with Powell Cottrille, he alerted us to a particular sighting of a Kirtland's by a friend of his at a spot slightly outside of the bird's designated territory. He gave us precise directions, and we pulled up at the side of the referenced dirt road late that Monday afternoon to listen for the bird, with hopes of at least seeing it.

We stood by the car and listened. Nothing. We drove down a little bit farther, stopped, and listened again. This time we heard the warbler, its song being a forceful combination of some low-pitched notes and high-pitched whistles. And stunningly, it was sitting right there in a small jack pine at the side of the road, singing and also carefully observing us. I fired three times before I realized that my flash wasn't attached. But not to worry. The bird, almost casually, moved but

Kirtland's Warbler (30), near Mio, Michigan, 1992

slightly over the next two minutes from the tree he was in to the very next tree not three feet away. In this picture-taking business, two minutes is a lifetime, and Vera and I were each able to photograph it well before the bird finally flew off. It was marvelous luck, and although the next morning on tour we saw several of these rare warblers, all of the "tour birds" had been banded with colored identification marks around their ankles, and the closest we were able to get to any one of them was about 50 feet. Our Kirtland's of the previous afternoon sang from 15 feet, and wore no jewelry at all.

The Kirtland's is a 4¾-inch bird, so deliberately plodding in its movements and so tame in its demeanor that you get the impression that it could almost be trained to eat from your hand. It seems at times almost petlike, but the bird also just happens to be the rarest warbler on the planet. Throughout history, there were probably never very many of them, but their numbers, until just recently, had crashed so precipitously that many feared the species would become extinct. In fact, at the low point of the Kirtland's population in the early 1970s, there were possibly no more than 15 pounds of this bird left in the world, the equivalent of about five good size ravens.

The Kirtland's makes its nest on the ground beneath the low limbs of a jack pine from six to nine feet tall. Since 1900, forest fires have been controlled to such an extent in this area that the trees grew too large to still be suitable for nest overhang, and no new trees were coming along to replace them. This loss of habitat was detrimental to the survival of the Kirtland's, granted, but it was the ravaging encroachment of the Brown-headed Cowbird that nearly did our little guy in. The cowbird was a bird of the short-grass prairies that moved into this area in the mid-1800s as the land was cut over for farmland. Since the Kirtland's had built up no evolutionary defenses against the cowbird, up to 70 percent of their nests were parasitized annually. Over the last few years, however, habitat has slowly been restored through the use of controlled burns, along with one recent "runaway" fire in the Upper Peninsula of Michigan that itself created thousands of acres of additional habitat for this bird. But the principal boost to the Kirtland's population has come from the proactive control of the cowbird itself through a trapping program that removes some 3,000 to 4,000 of these birds from the area each year. The effects have been dramatic, and the Kirtland's population has now grown to a 50-year high of approximately 1,300 birds. Although there may be some who think it unrighteous to eliminate even a few of one species though it may mean the full

Kirtland's Warbler, near Mio, Michigan, 1992

survival of another, most feel the ongoing health of this special bird from Michigan is dependent on periodic cowbird thinning.

Energized by our good fortune of being able to get close to the Kirtland's for a decent picture, we pressed on to Grayling, Michigan, where we had made plans to hook up with Bob Kemp, an extremely accomplished birder of the area. We had met Bob for the first time in the Andes of Ecuador as he was hitching a ride along a small dirt road, and we had stopped to give him a lift. We had been in the region to do some general rainforest photography, and had just returned from La Selva Lodge on the Napo River. We had only visited with Bob for a few hours at the time before he headed off on foot to explore the interior of another area, and we moved on to Quito for our flight back to the States. He had nevertheless encouraged us to look him up when we were up his way, so we had called him several weeks before our arrival to ask if he could do some prescouting work on some of the warblers we were after. Bob was a big help, and we were able to run down a variety of different birds that are indigenous to the area.

One in particular we will never forget—the Mourning Warbler (no. 31)—and it was Bob Kemp who put us right on it. We had been with Bob for a day and a half, and had seen a number of Golden-wingeds, Blue-wingeds, Waterthrushes, and such, when he announced that he had to head back to Grayling to finish a project on which he was currently working. Before he left, however, seemingly almost as an afterthought, he gave us directions to a particular location where a couple of years before he had seen a Mourning Warbler. His directions

Mourning Warbler (31), *near Grayling, Michigan, 1992*

were clear and on-point, but they led to a site that would have been the very last place in the state that Vera and I would have looked for this bird—the parking lot of the North Hillside Lake State Park in a wet glade area not 15 feet from its most conspicuous dumpster. But the bird was there, and we would remark later that this wasn't the first time we had found a rarity in an unlikely location. We heard the bird immediately after getting out of the car, and Vera and I walked right over to where he was singing. After this time making sure that our equipment was ready with both flashes and cameras properly set, Vera "pished." The bird flew directly to us, perching on a branch not 20 feet away to observe. We fired twice. The bird flew away. Vera "pished" again, and the bird flew in again. We fired twice more, and the bird flew away. Vera "pished" again—and so on, for several straight times. This was, in our experience, extremely unusual behavior, as we had found that most warblers might come to "pishing" just once, sometimes twice, but rarely more than that. Not only were we pleased to have had some good opportunities with this bird; we were also elated that he was such a handsome specimen.

Like the Connecticut and the MacGillivray's, this warbler is also a skulker that prefers tangled ravines and dense swamps and bogs. Unlike the Connecticut, which is a "walker," the Mourning, like the MacGillivray's, is a "hopper." The Mourning also looks different from the other two, in that it has an unusual and handsome black crepe "mourning" bib, and no eye ring at all. The Connecticut has a full eye ring, and the MacGillivray's has just a pair of white crescents, one above and one below each eye. The Mourning is fairly common in its range and breeds in Canada from British Columbia to Newfoundland, and in the United States from New England to the northern Midwest. It is, however, easier to hear than to see, and this lone male off the parking lot in a public park in Grayling, Michigan, was one of the few that Vera and I ever ran across. It was also the last of our 1992 birds, and it marked an upbeat end to our season. The trip to Minnesota, Wisconsin, and Michigan had been nine long days, and for all the birds we had seen, it was hard to believe that we had come away with only three keepers. But what keepers they were—the Connecticut, the Kirtland's, and the Mourning! These three warblers were considered by even the most experienced birders to be difficult targets to find and photograph, and having succeeded in finally capturing them, we felt we were legitimately on our way.

An Oregon Hermit, a Texas Ranger

ALTHOUGH we didn't know much about the Hermit Warbler, it was a bird that nevertheless worried us since it tended to nest and feed high in the spruce and fir forests of northern California and Oregon, and like the Connecticut Warbler we had seen only a few acceptable pictures of it through the years. We needed also to locate the Townsend's Warbler on this same trip since it too was known to nest in this general region. The Townsend's, however, was the more common of the two birds, and we consequently felt it would be the easier one for us to manage. We also reasoned that the common territory for these two warblers would overlap somewhere in northern Oregon, and there we would stand a good chance of connecting with both of them. We triangulated in on a little community on the eastern slopes of the Cascades called Sisters, Oregon, arrived there in mid-May 1993, and checked into the Lake Creek Lodge at Camp Sherman just up the road. The tourist season here wouldn't start for several weeks, and Vera and I had the place pretty much to ourselves except for Roblay McMullin, the elderly inhabitant of a little cottage across the stream from where we were staying. Roblay was a former owner of the lodge who had sold out several years before but still lived there under the terms of the sales contract.

Assisting in managing the lodge at the time was Lou Rens, himself an avid birder, and Vera and I spent the first morning with him, getting a feel for some of our tactical options, as well as trying to get a bead on the elusive MacGillivray's Warbler acknowledged to have been nesting in the thick brush a bit downstream from where we were staying. We were unsuccessful in locating that bird, but right after lunch we noticed another small bird working the foliage, warblerlike, just across the stream. We recognized it instantly as a Nashville Warbler (no. 32), a

Nashville Warbler (32), *Camp Sherman, Oregon, 1993*

bird we definitely needed, since all prior encounters with it during migration had failed to yield any appropriate photographs at all. Here it was on its nesting grounds, and we stood a better chance of enticing it to respond to tape. It did, just briefly and only once, and we were able to come away with a couple of acceptable shots. The Nashville is a common bird of the north woods that in many respects looks like a Connecticut Warbler with its breast painted yellow, although it is smaller than the Connecticut and has a completely different song.

Late that same afternoon, Roblay, whom we had not yet met nor even seen, called to us from across the stream to come join her for a drink. And thus began one of the most unusual episodes of our entire "warbler chasing" adventure. When she learned that Vera and I were from Texas, she paused momentarily, and then sallied forth with the following: "Before we settle in, there are three things you need to know: Number one—I've never been to Texas. Number two—I've never met a Texan. And Number three—quite frankly, I don't think I have missed a damn thing." We liked her immediately. Liked her a lot. She was salty and engaging as she wove tales of the colorful history of the Sisters/Bend communities. It was, however, about 45 minutes into the conversation, before she began to lean into her real agenda. She suggested that "since you two are from Texas, perhaps you would like to meet another Texan, Colonel Jack." When I asked her just who this Colonel Jack was, she invited us to look over our shoulders at a large oval oil painting of a bearded young man in buckskin kneeling on top of a rock ridge, gripping a rifle. The actual rifle itself hung beneath the painting. She said, "That's Colonel Jack Hays, Texas Ranger, and one of the heroes of the Mexican-American War." She went on to say that the painting memorialized an actual event in 1841 when Hays fended off a band of attacking Comanche from Enchanted Rock near Fredericksburg, Texas. The rifle beneath the painting was the one he presumably used that day.

We learned later that Jack Hays, a remarkable man by any measure, was commissioned by Sam Houston to form a "ranging" company in the 1840s to protect the settlements around San Antonio from the Comanche and other assorted renegades that were ravaging the area at the time. He particularly distinguished himself under the command of Zachary Taylor during the Mexican-American War, and afterward moved to California where he became sheriff of San Francisco County and the founder of Oakland, California. When I asked Roblay how she came by these marvelous possessions, she simply replied, "You see, I was married to the grandson of Colonel Jack Hays." Then in a manner that I acknowledged in retrospect was far more direct than it was polite, I asked her, "What do you plan to do with them?" She replied that she hadn't made any clear decision at that point, and we then began a discussion about the merits of leaving these historical possessions to the Texas Ranger Museum in Waco, Texas. After all, I explained, even Enchanted Rock itself was a famous Texas landmark originally preserved by the Nature Conservancy of Texas and now operated as a state park. Roblay twinkled a bit, smiled, and allowed as how there was some truth to what I was saying. A few weeks later, upon returning home, we were able to work out a bequest arrangement for these Hays possessions to return to Texas, which they did in August 1998 when Roblay passed away at the age of ninety-one.

Vera and I have not been back to Oregon, although we thought of Roblay often, exchanged cards, and talked on the phone every now and then. We also occasionally reflected back on that unusual confluence of

Audubon's Warbler (33), Suttle Lake, Oregon, 1993

circumstances, in some respects almost mystical in sweep, that drew us to Oregon where we had never been, to a little cottage owned by a little lady who had never been to Texas, but who nevertheless had hanging on her wall a remarkable piece of Texas Ranger legend. Vera and I know that future generations of Texans who visit Colonel Jack at the Ranger Museum there in Waco will owe Roblay McMullin a special debt of gratitude—for her generosity, to be sure, but also for her sense of rightness and order that, at the end of the day, as she set about to tidy up her own affairs, compelled her to simply do what she could to put things in their proper place.

The morning after our visit with Roblay, we headed up to Suttle Lake not far from Sisters and Camp Sherman and found it to be a delightful and picturesque spot to do our photography. Unfortunately, neither the birds nor the weather cooperated, and although we ran across several different warblers before noon, including a MacGillivray's, a Townsend's, and a Common Yellowthroat, we couldn't seem to get a decent shot. Then the rains came, and we spent the next two hours reading in the car, waiting for the weather to improve. It finally did, and as so often happens after a rain, the area became flooded with feeding birds trying to recoup precious foraging time. And there right in front of us not 10 feet from the parking lot, about midway up a mid-sized spruce, was an Audubon's Warbler (no. 33) going about his business. The rain had soaked his feathers, and the yellow markings on both wings as well as his head were extremely conspicuous. With his yellow throat he is easy to differentiate from his eastern counterpart, the Myrtle, which has a white throat. Additionally, the song of the Audubon's is more of a warble, while that of the Myrtle is more of a trill. One noteworthy similarity between these warblers is their habit of adding feathers to their nesting materials during springtime construction.

AN OREGON HERMIT, A TEXAS RANGER

Hermit Warbler (34), near Sisters, Oregon, 1993

Hermit Warbler, near Sisters, Oregon, 1993

The next morning we set out in earnest to try to find the real target of our trip to Oregon and the bird we had always expected to be one of the major obstacles to any goal of success, the Hermit Warbler. We decided to dedicate the day to thoroughly working the Indian Ford Creek area; and it was there in the ponderosa pine and juniper expanses that define this range that we found the Hermit (no. 34) as well as the Townsend's (no. 35), both on the very same morning. The Hermit and the Townsend's have closely related habitat, but the Hermit's song is characterized by high-pitched "see" notes, while that of the Townsend's has a buzzier "zee" quality, a lot like the Black-throated Green's of the fir and spruce forests of the East, and not all that dissimilar from the Golden-cheeked Warbler's of the Texas Hill Country. The Hermit usually nests below 5,000 feet, while the Townsend's generally prefers higher elevations. But here they both were at the same elevation along Indian Ford Creek, and we were able to photograph the two of them

Townsend's Warbler (35), near Sisters, Oregon, 1993

Townsend's Warbler, near Sisters, Oregon, 1993

MacGillivray's Warbler (36), near Sisters, Oregon, 1993

within 30 minutes of each other. The Hermit and the Townsend's are splendid birds, and Vera and I considered ourselves fortunate to have knocked off this "double" as easily as we had.

The last morning we were in Oregon, we decided to work our way back to the headwaters of the Metolius River, a place we had not yet explored, and there we picked up our last bird of this little Oregon adventure—the elusive MacGillivray's Warbler (no. 36). Very much like the Connecticut Warbler of the white eye ring, and the Mourning Warbler of the black crepe bib, this bird is also a low nester of the heavy brush, and is similarly difficult to approach. Vera and I were nevertheless fortunate with this bird, and Vera "pished" it right up on a log not 12 feet away. We were able to take one quick shot showing the telltale white crescents above and below each eye that differentiate this bird from the other two warblers. The MacGillivray's was the fifth warbler we had picked up here in Oregon, along with the Texas Ranger prize for the museum back home, and a brand-new friend in the redoubtable Roblay McMullin. The year 1993 had been a good one.

Little Girl Red
Little Boy Blue

AFTER our early 1994 migration stops on the Gulf Coast, Vera and I headed for the Chisos Mountains to look for the Colima Warbler, whose entire U.S. range is confined to a few hundred acres of montane woodland in the Big Bend area of Texas. Big Bend is a unique phenomenon of geography, as this impressive mountain range, with its attendant lush canyons, rises dramatically from the Chihuahuan desert floor. Although the Chisos are a long way from Dallas, the trip is nevertheless mandatory for finding the Colima in this country. Jim Peterson, who had explored the Chisos many times before, encouraged us to attack the more challenging Pinnacle Trail, rising directly out of Big Bend National Park to Boot Springs at the top. He advised that we wouldn't have any trouble finding the bird once we reached the correct elevation, no more than one hour up the side of the mountain. Four hours later, we dragged into Boot Springs having neither seen nor heard the bird at any point on the way up. Once we were at the top, however, we did manage some decent looks at several Colimas, but looks were all we could manage because we could get no closer than 35–40 feet to any one of them. After working the area for several hours trying to get near a singing perch, we called it a day and began the march back down the mountain empty-handed. The next day from Panther Pass we found another Colima on the Lost Mine Trail, but once again our opportunities were too distant to be productive. Bottom line: our first attempt for the Colima was a bust, and it was now time to move on into Arizona in search of several more of the warblers we needed there.

We pressed on through El Paso to southern Arizona in an effort to find the Virginia's Warbler, which we knew would also be one of the more difficult targets for us to photograph. In this assumption we were correct, and for three days we maneuvered up and down mountain

Lucy's Warbler (37), Santa Catalina Mountains, Arizona, 1994

trails in the Huachuca Mountains looking for this small, plain, elusive songbird. We were not successful. We covered Carr Canyon and Comfort Springs, worked the Nature Conservancy's Ramsey Canyon, and spent several hours on the Saw Mill Path of Garden Canyon. We saw many warblers, especially Painted Redstarts, but as for the Virginia's, we simply could not get close to the six or seven we were able to see to do us any good. As it turned out, the most impressive thing we encountered that week was the violent and erratic weather, and Vera and I spent a lot of afternoons dodging fast-moving, dark storms while at the same time marveling at the multiple rainbows and furious red sunsets they consistently spawned. Nevertheless, when we limped into Tucson at week's end, we were dispirited and cranky, for we had worked hard for six full days with nothing to show for it at all, and not all that many missed opportunities. But Tucson was the home of Rick Bowers, whom we had met on a trip to Belize a year earlier, and when we arrived in town he gave us advice and directions as to locating populations of Lucy's and Red-faced Warblers in areas just north of the city. Hopefully our luck would change.

At high noon the next day, it did. We were in Catalina State Park in the mesquite-covered foothills of the northwestern slope of the Santa Catalina Mountains. We were specifically after Lucy's Warbler (no. 37), and we were overrun by them. The Lucy's is one of the smallest of the warblers at just over four inches, and is the only warbler, other than

LITTLE GIRL RED/LITTLE BOY BLUE

Red-faced Warbler (38), Coronado National Forest, Arizona, 1994

the Prothonotary, to make its nest in a cavity. The Lucy's, more times than not, will choose an old mesquite tree, perhaps even using an abandoned woodpecker's or verdin's hole, and consequently this area was ideally suited for a nesting Lucy's. We saw many birds, but several hours passed before we were able to maneuver close enough to any one of them for a decent shot. But get one we did, and although we considered it only marginally acceptable, we nevertheless declared our slump over, and looked forward to the next day when we would try to find a Red-faced Warbler high up in the Coronado National Forest at Rose Canyon.

Traveling up Mount Lemmon in the Coronado National Forest the next morning, we started to hit ponderosa pines at about 7,000 feet along with songs from the resident warblers of this life zone: the Grace's, the Virginia's, and the Audubon's Warblers, and the Painted Redstart. We even got reasonably close to a singing Virginia's, but not close enough. At 8,000 feet we began to see white pine, Douglas fir, and aspen, and knew we were well into the habitat of the Red-faced Warbler when we pulled into Rose Canyon about 8 A.M.

It was to be the start of one of those marvelous, magical days that Vera and I would fondly look back on for years to come. The entire canyon, creek, and lake area were heavily populated with Red-faceds, and it was clearly the predominant warbler species of this particular habitat. We were able to get some reasonably good shots of some feeding birds early but still had not gotten close enough to be completely satisfied. About 11 A.M. we climbed the back side of a small hill where we could see a couple of Red-faceds foraging, but they moved off as we approached the area. We stopped to rest a bit from the climb and, about a minute later, looked up to observe the same two birds slowly moving our way, deliberately feeding as they approached closer and closer. We remained motionless, afraid to stir. They worked to about 15 feet from us, and we were able to take two shots before they backed off. Thirty seconds later they approached us slowly again, and what we determined to be the female came just a little closer to us than before. Both the male and female Red-faced, like most Mexican warblers, look pretty much the same, but it seemed to us that the male may have been a little brighter, with a head that looked more cleanly helmeted.

Then Vera did an unusual thing. In extremely soft tones, very much as a mother would talk to a baby, she began to coax the female to come closer. The bird obliged, moving to within five to six feet of where Vera was now sitting on the ground. The warbler was actually too close for

Vera to focus on, and she had to wait for it to move back a bit before she could even shoot. Vera would then snap a picture, the bird would move off several feet, Vera would resume her coaxing routine, and the bird would again work closer into range. It was an amazing thing to watch. It was also apparent that there must be a nest nearby, hence the extreme fearlessness of this mother bird in particular. After about 10 minutes, and many marvelous opportunities for photographs, we backed away to see if, in fact, there was a nest in the vicinity. We were also careful in our retreat to avoid stepping on anything that might resemble such a possibility. Almost immediately, our suspicions were confirmed as the female headed right for a small indentation in the ground underneath a large root of a Douglas fir, close to where we had been standing. We concluded that eggs must be on the nest, and we permanently left the area so as to prevent any chance of abandonment.

I personally considered the Red-faced to be a magnificent little bird, one of the most unusually colorful of any of our warblers; but Vera,

Red-faced Warbler, Coronado National Forest, Arizona, 1994

Red-faced Warbler, Coronado National Forest, Arizona 1994

charmed once again with an altogether different degree of sensitivity, felt she had to name it. So our little Red-faced female (no. 38) thus became "Little Girl Red." It was as close as we were ever to get to any one of the warblers we were after, and we were able to observe it and its behavior at relative leisure. This bird is one of the Mexican varieties, like the Painted Redstart, the Olive, and the Grace's, that have carved out southeastern Arizona and southwestern New Mexico as the northernmost part of their nesting range. No warbler—make that no bird—looks quite like a Red-faced, and we were pleased to have gotten excellent shots of it. Some of our best.

The day wasn't over, however, and we were still enthusiastically reliving our encounter with "Little Girl Red" when I thought I heard the trill-ending song of the Grace's Warbler (no. 39) coming from the top of a large Ponderosa Pine at the edge of the lake. I hurriedly fished in

Grace's Warbler (39), *Coronado National Forest, Arizona, 1994*

Grace's Warbler, Coronado National Forest, Arizona, 1994

Black-throated Blue Warbler (40), *near Bluefield, Virginia, 1994*

my bag for the tape of the Grace's, found it, and gave it a toot. It immediately spiraled down to within 12 feet from where we were standing, and we nailed it. Over the past several years, we had heard the song of the Grace's many times in southeast Arizona, played the tape of that song many of those same times, but today was the first instance that this warbler had responded in such a dramatic way. It once again proved to us that while some birds respond occasionally to the tape, it is never a sure bet that any particular bird will do so. With the Grace's we were lucky, and using the tape enabled us finally to get close to this bird. The Grace's Warbler is also a pretty bird, in many ways similar in appearance and habits to the Yellow-throated Warbler of the large pine forests of the South. This warbler would also wind up being the last warbler we would photograph in Arizona, as we were now headed east, to track down quarry peculiar to the hills and ridges of West Virginia.

LITTLE GIRL RED/LITTLE BOY BLUE

We arrived in West Virginia on May 20 at Pipestem State Park a bit due east of Princeton, and worked the area hard for several days with the help of Jim Phillips, the park superintendent. We saw and heard many of the birds we were specifically after, including the Worm-eating and Cerulean Warblers, the Louisiana Waterthrush, and the Ovenbird. For the life of us, though, we could not get anything to work, and we began to conclude that we were too late into the season. The birds had most likely already staked out their territories, picked their mates, and were not as responsive as we usually found them to be at the beginning of the season when they were fighting to establish territorial rights. After four days of hard work, we were discouraged, because although we could hear and see many of the birds, we couldn't get a one to respond or come close to us in any way. In the afternoon of the fourth day, we decided to explore the East River Mountain area near Bluefield, West Virginia. As we moved up the mountain, we were impressed with the large, mature stands of cucumber magnolia and white oak trees, but saw little in the way of bird life. We crossed the top and were heading down to the Virginia side when we began to notice increasingly large stands of rhododendron. Although this happens to be ideal habitat for the Black-throated Blue Warbler, we had not heard a one sing on either side of the mountain. With nothing much to lose, however, I walked to the edge of the road, played the tape of the bird's song, and waited. Nothing. I played it again. Again, nothing. I had turned to leave, when I was startled by some small movement off to my right. Sure enough, it was him—the male Black-throated Blue (no. 40)—and he was right on top of me. This set the tone for the rest of the afternoon, as we slowly worked down the back side of East River Mountain, playing the tape at every large stand of rhododendron we found, kicking up Black-throated Blues at every turn, and racking up good shots of this terrific bird. What the Prothonotary Warbler is to Vera, the Black-throated Blue is to me—it is my favorite warbler. One reason that I like the bird so much has to do with its unusual coloration, not only the colors themselves—blue, black, and white—but also the way they neatly fit together. The colors don't bleed into one another, but stop crisply at the border. The female looks nothing like the male, being a soft, olive green with telltale white patches on the wings; years back it was even believed to have been a separate species entirely. The Black-throated Blue has a lot to recommend it in that it is relatively easy to approach and see as it nests and feeds low in the laurel, evergreen, and rhododendron habitat that it prefers. It is also usually monogamous, it helps the female build her nest, dutifully feeds her while she is on it, and finally helps feed the nestlings when they are hatched. So, exhilarated from this our first success of the week, Vera, waxing enchanted, did her naming thing. This time it was "Little Boy Blue."

The next morning we explored the New River Gorge area in Summers County and took the winding dirt road down to the Crumps Bottom drainage near Bull Falls. This is an amazing area for birds in general and warblers in particular; even a Sutton's Warbler, a rare cross between a Parula and a Yellow-throated, has been documented here. We saw nothing that exotic, although we were fortunate to find, for our first time ever, the unusual nest of the Ovenbird. This nest is a domed structure, very much like the "Dutch Oven" for which the bird is named. Vera and I had heard the song of this bird—"teacher, teacher, teacher"—all the way from Minnesota to Pennsylvania to Virginia, but the only time we had ever had a good look at one was when we encountered it on migration. Then it is particularly easy to approach. The bird

Black-throated Blue Warbler, Blacksburg, Virginia, 1995

Black-throated Blue Warbler, Blowing Rock, North Carolina, 1995

reminds one of a small thrush in its looks and behavior as it slowly patrols its turf, bobbing at times, turning over leaves and high-stepping over the forest floor in its search for food. Here at Bull Falls, as we crouched motionless a discreet distance from the nest full of babies, we were able to observe it at leisure. We were also fortunate enough an hour or so later to find a singing male, and the Ovenbird became no. 41.

Two other warblers that also seem more like thrushes than warblers are appropriately named the Northern Waterthrush and the Louisiana Waterthrush. They are extremely similar in both looks and behavior, although some very slight variations exist in that the Northern has a more even eyeline and flesh-colored legs while the Louisiana has an increasingly wider white eyeline that flares behind the eye and pink legs. The Northern has a spotted throat; the Louisiana, a longer bill. They both nest and feed low, and bob their tails as they walk. Side by side it is reasonably easy to tell them apart, but they are rarely side by side. The Louisiana migrates to the United States early and prefers the fast-

Ovenbird (41), Summers County, West Virginia, 1994

moving streams and rivers of the South. The Northern comes later and marks its habitat as the slower moving waters and ravines of the North.

Although we had encountered the bird on migration with regularity, as well as in a number of different regions of the North, Vera picked up our most suitable pictures of the Northern Waterthrush (no. 42) while at its wintering home in Belize. She was staying for several days at the famous rainforest lodge, Chan-Chich, near Gallon Jug, doing some general photography of the tropical birds of the area, including motmots, toucans, and trogons. While there, she had the opportunity to try for a wintering Northern Waterthrush that she heard working the bank on the other side of a dark creek. On their wintering grounds, these birds are often easy to find, but they are nevertheless hard to get close to because they have no established nesting territory and consequently do not respond to tape recordings. Our best chance was to get near them when they were feeding, much like this Northern was doing near the Chan-Chich lodge. Vera could not get across the creek to the bird, but she noticed a large bare-limbed sapling about 20 feet out in the middle of the creek. Realizing that she would most likely have but one chance at the warbler, she waded stealthily into the creek, carefully prefocused on the sapling, and set herself up for a possible photograph. She then "pished" once and the Northern blew into the sapling for a look. Vera fired once. It moved a couple of feet out on the branch; Vera fired again. Then it flew to the bank nearby and she fired successfully for the last time.

LITTLE GIRL RED/LITTLE BOY BLUE

The next spring in early April we looked for the Louisiana Waterthrush on its linear territory in the hardwood bottomlands alongside the Angelina River near Nacogdoches, Texas. We were with our friend David Wolf, with whom we had previously spent some time both in the Hato Pinero region of Venezuela as well as La Selva on the Napo River in Ecuador. David's home is Nacogdoches, right in the midst of

Northern Waterthrush (42), *near Gallon Jug, Belize, 1994*

Louisiana Waterthrush (43), *near Nacogdoches, Texas, 1995*

excellent habitat for the Louisiana, and we were confident that he could put us right on one. We heard it first, a song that was musical, loud, and high-pitched. It was nearly as impressive as that of the Swainson's, and David likened it to a "falling cascade." When he played back its song, the bird came in briefly for a look, just long enough for Vera to get our first and only shot of the Louisiana Waterthrush (no. 43). Then the bird was off—well before we could really determine if his legs were flesh colored or pink, or if the eyeline was narrow or wide. But it was here in the South, it was early April, the river was fast moving, and the bird was singing on territory. And David Wolf, the expert, had no doubts about the song: a Louisiana, for sure.

From Mexico to Manitoba

IT'S been pretty much accepted that getting photographs of 35 warblers is reasonably easy and that photographing 45, if you have four or five good seasons to do it, is also achievable. But capturing all 52 of the non-hybrid warblers that regularly nest in this country is difficult—at least it was for us. Bringing in the last of these special birds required some tactical adjustments, schedule realignments, and ample measures of luck in 1995 and 1996.

The final leg of our journey began oddly enough in pursuit of a bird that had not even been on our targeted list of warblers at the beginning. It was a bird that Vera and I had not considered to be one of the wood warblers that habitually nested in the United States—the Tropical Parula. Admittedly, we knew that some had been seen in South Texas in Kenedy County, but we had interpreted these to be more or less episodic sightings and hadn't considered it further. However, over dinner one night during the summer of 1994, Jim Peterson annoyingly set us straight. He was adamant that Tropical Parulas regularly nested in South Texas, although he admitted there weren't all that many birds in aggregate. He felt that if we were to stake any claim to having gotten all of the non-hybrid U.S. warblers, then the Tropical Parula must be included. This was not welcome news, and we automatically assumed that Peterson was chasing nits to pick. After only a little research, however, we reluctantly concluded that he was right and grudgingly added the Tropical Parula to our list.

Where to find it was another question. A few birds dancing in an obscure oak motte somewhere in South Texas didn't seem all that promising, so we turned to Victor Emanuel for advice. Victor suggested we abandon the notion of trying to locate the bird in the United States and redirect our efforts to the place where the bird was far more

Tropical Parula (44), *Picachos Mountains, Mexico, 1995*

common—northern Mexico. He put us in touch with friends of his, Andrés and Pilar Sada, a marvelous couple of old-world charm from Monterrey who happened to be the most accomplished birders in all of Mexico. Andrés had identified 951 birds in Mexico and was ranked no. 1 in his country, and Pilar had tallied an impressive 915 and was ranked no. 2! They graciously invited us to their weekend home about an hour and a half north of Monterrey in the Picachos Mountains. It was hands down one of the loveliest places we had ever been, with canyons of pine and sycamore and ancient oaks laden with Spanish moss. The bird life was phenomenal. Some of the species seen just from their terrace, over cocktails no less, included Wild Turkey, Varied Bunting,

Acorn Woodpecker, Green Jay, Rose-throated Becard, Elegant Trogon, several species of orioles, and a Summer Tanager.

And of course, there were Tropical Parulas (no. 44). Tons of them. It was as large a population of any of the warblers we were to encounter, and in two days we must have jumped no less than 20 singing males. We were in the northern part of their range, which runs all the way from Texas to Uruguay and Argentina, and these tropicals were attracted to this oasis of oak and Spanish moss as preferred nesting habitat. The bird itself is similar in size and behavior to the Northern Parula we regularly found in the cypress and tupelo stands of Caddo Lake.

Although both birds have similar songs, built around a rising, buzzy trill, there are some distinctive differences in the way they look. The

Tropical Parula, Picachos Mountains, Mexico, 1995

Northern has white eye crescents; the Tropical has a black eye-mask. The difference is significant, making the Northern look alert and sweet, and the Tropical somewhat sinister. Also, the Northern has a rust colored breast band, while the Tropical has a yellow-orange breast. A couple of years later on the Norias Division of the King Ranch in South Texas, Vera and I had another encounter with a unique subspecies of the same bird. We were with Helen Alexander of the King Ranch family, when we jumped a Tropical Parula in one of the large

Orange-crowned Warbler (45), *Picachos Mountains, Mexico, 1995*

Canada Warbler (46), near Blacksburg, Virginia, 1995

oak mottes there that had the usual Tropical markings, but also carried small, split white eye rings common to the Northern Parula. We initially thought it was some rare hybrid, but later determined it was simply a subspecies of the Tropical not all that unusual in the area.

Also in the Picachos, there was a dividend—an Orange-crowned Warbler feeding here on its wintering grounds each morning in stands of huisache and white thorn acacia. A bird of western North America that breeds all the way north through Canada to Alaska, the Orange-crowned Warbler is most easily recognized, in fact, by its absolute lack of distinguishing characteristics or field marks of any kind. It is a uniformly dull olive all over. As for the "orange crown" feature, it should be labeled more fiction than fact, for it is rarely seen and is of no benefit whatsoever in the field in trying to identify one. However, we tiptoed up to an Orange-crowned Warbler (no. 45) one morning as it was busily feeding and snapped its picture. It was no more difficult than that. Thus, in addition to snaring the special bird of the Picachos, the

Canada Warbler, Point Pelee, Ontario, 1995

Tropical Parula, we now had the Orange-crowned as well, along with two new friends from Monterrey.

That same spring, Vera and I had the opportunity to go back to Virginia to search specifically for the Worm-eating Warbler and the Canada Warbler, as well as a possible upgrade or two of the Golden-winged. We were only partially successful. Our first stop was the Mountain Lake Hotel near Blacksburg, Virginia, known more widely for having been the location for the movie Dirty Dancing than for being home to populations of nesting wood warblers. We saw quite a few birds including good numbers of Black-throated Blues and Kentuckys, as well as a pair of Canadas, a bird that up to this point we had not been able to photograph adequately. However, on this trip we were more successful, and we ambushed a couple along a fern-lined creek not far from the hotel on the back side of the lake. One, in particular, responded well to tape, and the Canada Warbler became bird no. 46. The Canada is a bird of the dense understory and this creekbed where we found it represented ideal habitat for the species. It nests in the heavy woods of the North through Canada and is easily recognized by two telltale features: distinct yellow "spectacles," and a "black necklace." Dead giveaways. The Canada is also impressive in its aerial displays, and several times while we were observing this bird it sallied forth quite athletically in pursuit of its prey, each time with effortless success. It was said of DiMaggio that he made the hard ones look easy; the Canada does it that way too.

The next morning, we headed over to the Kemberling Creek Bridge near Pearisberg to look for Golden-wingeds in meadows adjoining part of the Appalachian Trail, but we were not successful. In the afternoon we drifted over near Pandampas Pond, where we saw Ovenbirds, a Worm-eating Warbler, and an American Redstart, but again no photographic success. So we left Virginia, and headed north through Bluefield, West Virginia, where we had been the year before, on over to Bolt Mountain for a rendezvous scheduled for the next morning with a charming naturalist of the area named Dolly Stover. Dolly had for several years been overseeing a banding project of Golden-winged Warblers in some reclaimed coal mining areas on the back side of Bolt Mountain, and we were hopeful that with her we would have some luck there. This region was what one might call "mountain man" country, clearly not suited for drugstore cowboys or middle-aged dropouts with ponytails. There were no gentrified "olde shoppes" on Bolt Mountain, and Starbuck's house blends had not yet invaded the higher elevations.

We met Dolly the next morning, along with her husband, Ernest, and were escorted to an abandoned and reclaimed mining operation owned by Pittston Coal. We then entered a world of tangles and scarps and reclaimed ridges that were completely overgrown and wild. Dolly and Ernest took us deep into its maw about three miles or so, with the plan that we would slowly work our way out through the afternoon back to our car left at the entrance.

Ernest was unquestionably a mountain man, built solid and low to the ground. He only spoke to us twice the entire morning—the first when we were initially introduced; the second when he and Dolly were about to leave us, and he casually asked, "Are you carrying a gun?" The question hit us hard, since "gun" was not on our check-list of required equipment for "hunting" warblers. I mumbled a no, and then asked why he thought we needed one. In his slow mountain drawl he said that there were five things he would worry about, if he were us: "snakes, wild dogs, wild boar, black bear," and then the clincher, "escaped convicts." This was not fun news, but Ernest's tone seemed

Yellow-breasted Chat (47), Bolt Mountain, West Virginia, 1995

suspiciously more designed to rattle city slickers than to signal any real danger. At any rate, we decided to suck it up and stay the course—without a gun and brandishing only an aluminum monopod as a modest form of low-tech protection.

As it turned out, we didn't need a gun that day, but we could have used a longer lens to get closer to the Golden-wingeds we flushed all afternoon. Golden-wingeds were all over the place, and we must have seen at least 10 males within a very narrow area of coverage. There were so many of the birds, with what appeared to be overlapping territories, that songs were coming from all directions. Consequently, the seductive sounds from our own tape produced a gigantic and collective yawn. Bottom line: no Golden-wingeds, and no escaped convicts, as we were menaced only by the nagging disappointment of a splendid opportunity missed, an important and clearly hittable target unhit. It was a tough afternoon, although it was an excellent birding location, and we heard and saw Hoodeds, Black-throated Greens, Kentuckys, Ceruleans,

Tennessee Warbler (48), *Thompson, Manitoba, 1995*

Indigo Buntings, and a magnificent Scarlet Tanager. But no warbler photographs, until rather late in the day as we were heading back toward our car and heard the unmistakable song of the Yellow-breasted Chat. It was an excellent specimen, but at first we thought we were out of luck since I had no Chat tape with me, not having expected to try for this bird in West Virginia. But remembering a trick I had learned from Andrés Sada, I pulled out a small, plastic oil funnel, in the throat of which I had already placed a small microphone that was plugged in to the tape recorder. I then recorded the live sound of the singing Chat and played his own song back to him. This somewhat desperate attempt worked far better than I had any right to expect, and the bird flew in close to check us out in a series of maneuvers that were marvelous in both scope and execution. He charged, skulked low in the brush, floated from limb to limb, and finally after one of his many territorial songs, puffed up his neck and jutted out his beard much like the Golden-collared Manakins on their leks in the rainforests of Central America. It was in this manner that we were able to get our first pictures of the Yellow-breasted Chat (no. 47), although it is a bird we had seen many times before all over the country and was in fact a common resident of the overgrown fields of East Texas. It also seemed a bit absurd that with this bird nesting as close by as an hour from our home that we would have to go all the way to West Virginia to get its picture.

The Yellow-breasted Chat is an unusual bird; but it is an outrageous warbler. If warblers were ever to form an exclusive club or fraternity, the first thing they would do is vote to keep the Chat out. It's too big, it's too loud, and it's way too different. A bird that is found in the dense undergrowth of secondary habitat in practically every state, the Chat at 7 1/2 inches is nearly twice as long as other warblers. Whereas most warblers don't have much of an imposing song and sound more like insects than birds, the Chat is extremely loud and versatile. It doesn't sound like a warbler at all, but more like an awkward cross between a catbird and a mockingbird, with a song filled with a mixture of chucks and whistles, rattles and mews. One hears them all the time, but they are seen less frequently. This was the first time that Vera and I had gotten close enough to this peculiar creature—one that ornithologists still claim with a straight face is a warbler—to get a decent shot. So instead of Texas, where we had always taken for granted that we would capture the Chat, we were ultimately successful here on this reclaimed ridge on Bolt Mountain.

Heading back toward Richmond the next day, we ventured down the

Blue Ridge Parkway to signpost 79, a few miles from Peaks at Otter, and took an aptly named stretch called Warbler Road, where we surprised a couple of Ceruleans in a stand of large tulip trees, but were not successful in getting close to either one. We also found two different male Worm-eating Warblers on the wooded hillsides coming down the mountain, but were still unsuccessful, so we decided to flee West Virginia to try something else.

The next bird we needed to track down was the Tennessee Warbler, and although we had seen this bird many times on migration, we knew that we would have to go into the heart of its nesting territory to get close enough to it for an acceptable photograph. The bird's range runs about as far north as one can go, but on the advice of Kim Eckert, we nevertheless headed for Thompson, Manitoba. It's worth emphasizing that one doesn't just stumble into Thompson looking for something to do, as it has all the charm of a small East European town shortly after World War II. It also has the feel of a town under siege, as forest fires rage all around the area on an annual basis, and the surrounding countryside is still decorated with the charred stalks of the "big one" of 1989. Adding to the otherworldly flavor of the place is the impression that very few of the streets seemed to connect with one another, and we spent a lot of time making turns but advancing very little. But Thompson is the true gateway to the north. If you are interested in visiting INCO's big nickel plant, you come here; or if you are on the second leg of the popular eco-tour that goes to Churchill for polar bear in the winter and nesting godwits and curlews in the summer; or if, like us, you just happen to be looking for Tennessee Warblers.

We found them where we thought we would at Paint Lake, and it wasn't difficult because the bird's song is loud, high-pitched, and constant. The Tennessee is relatively plain by comparison to most warblers but is nevertheless handsome in its own way—with an olive back, gray head, white eyeline, and snow-white undercarriage. It looks to most of us a lot like a vireo. Although there is nothing particularly unusual about its behavior, this warbler is at times prone to feast on berries of all kinds, as well as grapes. The love of the grape has at times led this warbler to ravage vineyards on its fall migration south, and drunk October Tennessees are not all that rare. The best bird we found was a stone-sober and aggressive male in unremarkable habitat next to a rutted maintenance road at the local golf course. Thus it was here in Thompson, a two-hour flight north of Winnipeg, that we finally knocked down the Tennessee (no. 48). Then we beat it out of town.

After Thompson, Manitoba, and pretty much as an afterthought, we headed for the Riding Mountain National Forest, about a 2 1/2-hour drive due west of Winnipeg, to run down whatever warblers we could find in the area. This is where the lush June-green farmland of southern Manitoba uplifts into the higher elevations of white spruce, aspen, fir, and jack pine. We easily nestled in at the Mooswa Lodge in a little town called Wassagaming, which is the Ojibwa Indian name for "clear lake." We did not do well with our warblers here, and we did not pick up even a slight upgrade. But we had a magnificent time nevertheless because of the extraordinary other wildlife of the forest there. Vera and I had never seen anything remotely like it. Our memories of Wassagaming will always be laced with images of strutting Spruce Grouse on their lek at dawn; a drumming Ruffed Grouse perched proud on a log, sounding like a diesel engine revving up for the day; the magnificent Great Gray Owl on her nightly vole hunt two miles up the road; the lone loon and lone beaver at Clear Lake making their nightly patrols; the female Black Bear and her three cubs; the fearless Coyote up near Bead Lake; and of course, the moose. There were moose all over the place from cow to calf to velvet-horned bulls. We had never seen so much wildlife anywhere in North America, and we were equally amazed that we had never even heard of this place before.

Also while in Wassagaming, we ran across Bob Ridgely and Guy Tudor, the famous author and illustrator of the four-volume set of *The Birds of South America*, the first two of which have already been published. They were in town on a field trip sponsored by the Philadelphia Academy of Natural Sciences, and were on their way to Churchill. Ridgely is one of the great naturalists and ornithologists of our time, a legend in the field of Central and South American birding. He has, as one might say, "written the book," and in early 1998 even discovered a new species of tropical bird in the Andes of Ecuador, an antpitta heretofore unknown to science. Like Steve Hilty, John O'Neill, and the late Ted Parker, these men represented the acknowledged best of tropical birding, yet they were all raised and educated in the United States. Although here we all were in the north woods of Canada, we surprisingly didn't spend any time discussing the wildlife of Manitoba, or even the resident wood warblers of the area, for that matter. Our entire conversation centered around rainforest birds in general, and an uncommonly rare bird of the neotropics in particular that was of special interest to Ridgely—namely, the Rufous-vented Ground-Cuckoo. Ridgely had seen this bird (which resembles a remarkably handsome,

Tennessee Warbler, Thompson, Manitoba, 1995

giant roadrunner) only a few times during a long career of neotropical birding, and he maintained that the bird had never been properly photographed. Coincidentally, Vera and I had lucked into this very same bird a couple of years before and had taken an acceptably decent picture of it as it was busy stalking an army ant swarm in a remote area of southern Panama called the Darien.

The Darien is actually renowned for some of the most extraordinary ant swarms in all the neotropics, with sometimes up to one million ants participating. These Darien swarms also attract one of the largest varieties of antbird followings anywhere, with occasionally up to 8–10 different species of these birds involved.

These antbirds, however, are attracted to ant swarms not in order to eat the ants, but simply to follow them. They are only after the other insects that have been panicked by the onslaught sweeping the forest floor. Millipedes, scorpions, katydids, and cockroaches scurry to escape the foray, only to then be picked off by these bands of antbirds that have been stalking the swarm, waiting for just such a moment.

Although there are many species of antbirds in the tropics, only a few are actually considered to be "professional" ant-swarm followers. Some of these "pros" have become so specialized to this process that they do not know how to forage for prey in any other way and are entirely dependent on the ant swarm for survival. More times than not, you can hear these birds long before you actually discover the swarm itself, as they chatter and churr, scold and whistle, while they jockey and spar for strategic positions and perches to best harvest the fallout from the attack.

The army ants are, in fact, ferocious biters and stingers, but Vera and I had discovered that they would not climb up our rubber boots, so intently focused were they on the strong scent laid down by the ants that had preceded them, and so unappetizing in both smell and texture were the boots themselves. Although neither of us were particularly inclined toward reckless behavior, or even the therapy of a cheap thrill, we felt that standing in the swarm itself was a manageable risk—so we took a deep breath, and waded in. Among perhaps a million ants. Not because we particularly relished the idea, but because that's where these magnificent and interesting birds were actively performing. Vera moved into the swarm with a certain degree of grace; I stumbled in more on the order of "El Tapir." We positioned ourselves up toward the front of the movement where most of the action was predictably occurring, and it was here that the magic slowly began to unfold. We stood very still, and watched. And then over the ensuing 15 minutes, as the ants continued to move steadily over our boots, the birds themselves began to move in closer to where we were standing, becoming more intently riveted to runaway insects and less and less concerned with our presence. We took photographs of woodcreepers and manakins, antthrushes and motmots. We shot within 10 feet of the Bicolored and Ocellated Antbirds, got a marvelous picture of the splendid Black-crowned Antpitta, and finally at about 20 feet, nailed the big, rare cuckoo. It was a banner afternoon, very much on par with some of those sensational fallout mornings at High Island, and one of those magical experiences that nature every now and then sends your way. And we weren't stung or bitten once!

It was a privilege for us to be able to compare notes on neotropical birding with experts like Ridgely and Tudor, and we hoped that we would run into them again. But Manitoba had ended our warbler season for 1995, and the next year we were going to have to "pump some iron" to get the rest.

And Finally—Colima

OUR first stop in 1996 was in the Ozarks of Arkansas, which we had circled primarily for a run at the Worm-eating Warbler, since we had previously been unsuccessful with this bird in Connecticut, West Virginia, and even on the Texas Coast. Most Texans never travel to the Ozarks, and it's a shame, because the Ozarks are magnificent most any time of year and stack up every bit as well as some of the more fashionable mountain habitats in Colorado and New Mexico. The roads are also in good shape, and the only thing "hillbilly" we found in northwestern Arkansas was the occasional siren song to tourists to come visit "Booger Hollow" and the like.

We hooked up with John Andre of the U.S. Forest Service out of Hector, who was very knowledgeable of the birds of the area. He took us to a particular spot where for the last several years he had heard a singing Worm-eating Warbler. Off Route 27, paralleling the Illinois Bayou River, back on a wooded hillside that dropped fast to big rocks and then to a creek, we first heard, then saw, and then photographed the Worm-eating Warbler (no. 49). This bird is another low nester of the ravines and wooded hillsides of a range that runs through the central United States from Arkansas to New England. It is a "hopper" rather than a "walker," searches the ground leaves for insects, which it much prefers to "worms," and sings a song that sounds very much like that of a Chipping Sparrow. Vera and I have always liked the Worm-eating Warbler, for its low feeding behavior to be sure, but primarily because of the way it looks. From field guides and bird books this declaration might seem faintly comic, as the bird appears on the illustrated page to be somewhat drab. But it is not. It has a light cinnamon or rich buff color with two black head stripes, which makes it legiti-

Worm-eating Warbler (49), *Ozark National Forest, Arkansas, 1996*

mately handsome to most who see it up close. This warbler had been a favorite of ours for some time, and is also much fancied by serious birders.

The next day, in further search of Worm-eatings, as we came down the backside of a mountain south of Sand Gap, we heard the buzzy, telltale song of a Blue-winged Warbler coming from a stretch of secondary growth at the bottom. The Ozarks represent the southwestern extent of this bird's range, which runs through the Midwest to New England. The Blue-winged prefers the habitat of abandoned pastures and upland clearings, and where its range overlaps with that of the Golden-winged, the Blue-winged seems to always to prevail, thus driving the Golden-winged away. This has become increasingly worrisome as the Blue-winged species advances each year farther north, and the population of Golden-wingeds are annually tabulated to be less in number than the year before. This particular Blue-winged was the only one Vera and I saw while in Arkansas, and it may well have been an isolated, lonely male, randy yet doomed to bachelorhood, way out on the far edge of its range. When we played back its two-note, buzzy song, it blew in to about 12 feet, and we were able to get some close-up shots, which showed the telltale markings of bluish gray wings on a full yellow bird, with a black streak running through each eye. Although we had come to the Ozarks for the Worm-eating, in particular, the Blue-winged was a welcome dividend. It was also bird no. 50; two more to go.

AND FINALLY—COLIMA

Warbler no. 51 was to be the Virginia's, which we had unsuccessfully tracked, first in the scrub oak coming down from Rustler Park at Cave Creek, Arizona, then the next year in Carr Canyon northwest of there toward Tucson, and finally in Ramsey Canyon near Carr. It was a tough bird in almost every respect. It didn't cross water on migration, and finding its nest was considered to be almost an impossibility; some ornithologists had tried for years to do so, without success. We didn't even try. We also had concluded that the bird didn't respond all that

Worm-eating Warbler, Sabine Woods, Texas, 1997

well to tape, either to its own song or to that of a local owl. Finally, we had even struck out when trying to get close to one of its singing perches. Admittedly, we had not yet tried a water drip in an arid part of its habitat, nor attempted to run it down on its wintering grounds on the west coast of Mexico, nor even come to its nesting grounds while it was feeding its young. We had also not really worked it hard in an area of its range where it was presumably the most prevalent—the Gambel oak canyons of Colorado. So it was there we went next, specifically to Colorado Springs to find this elusive warbler.

If you actively pursue warblers around the United States, you will see incredible variety in our nation's countryside, run across stunning samples of its best wildlife, and additionally meet some nice and interesting people. You will not, however, dine often in fine restaurants or stay in upscale places. This project was about beautiful and elusive small birds; it was also about greasy food on back roads in down-market diners. Wild birds don't consistently hang out around five-star hotels, but Colorado Springs was a rare exception. There we were able to stay in the charming Garden of the Gods Club owned by our

Blue-winged Warbler (50), *Ozark National Forest, Arkansas, 1996*

Virginia's Warbler (51), *Durango, Colorado, 1996*

good friends, the Margaret Hill family out of Dallas. The panoramic views here are some of the best in the country, and we also enjoyed both the food and the accommodations in the golf cottages across from the club facilities. We were not able to take in the golf, however, because we were up early every morning and on our way south to work the Nature Conservancy preserve at Akin Canyon, the San Isabel Mountains south of Wetmore, and Espinosa Gulch just north of Canyon City. But to no avail. Nothing. Sure, we saw a few birds, but we just couldn't get close enough for a good photograph, and this small, gray bird stays well concealed even when you are able to get mathematically near it. After a few days of a very hard and exhausting effort, we decided we needed to try something different in a new locale. Fortunately, we had done some preliminary homework and had a backup plan of sorts, and so we drove six hours across the state to Durango, and the Bodo State Wildlife Area nearby. Although we were disappointed in the overall habitat of the area, as there were not the large stands of Gambel oak that we had expected, we did run across one good section of these trees on the east side of the Animas River at its junction with Wildcat Canyon Road. Here, after chasing this bird for nearly three years, for a total of about 10 different days, we finally got a photograph of the Virginia's Warbler (no. 51). It responded to tape, when perhaps 25 others that had preceded it had not, only for an instant but close enough for us to connect for a picture. It was not a great picture, just good enough to tell that it's definitely a Virginia's, and the adage proved true—that a homely bird sought hard can at times mean more than a glorious one taken easily. This mousy little warbler that we finally found in the Gambel oaks at 5,000 feet near Durango—as plain as this bird was, and as lackluster as our shot of it was—brought delight and a certain measure of relief to Vera and me. Warbler no. 51 was in the bag.

Now we had but one to go—the Colima, found at the top of the Chisos Mountains in the Big Bend area of Texas. In 1994 we had climbed up to Boot Springs to photograph it but had come away empty-handed. In 1995 we had taken a different tack, and had looked for the bird with Andrés Sada in the lower elevations of some ranch canyons near Saltillo, Mexico. We saw several of the birds on that trip, but there was a terrible drought in northern Mexico at the time, and the birds seemed listless and did not sing. They were not at all responsive to us, and we had come away from our second attempt at the Colima with no photograph to show for it at all. In two days there, we hadn't fired a shot.

In the spring of 1996 we decided to try the Saltillo area again, and this time we were aided by the advice and detailed area maps provided us by the noted Texas birder Greg Lasley, who had thoroughly explored the area several years before. Saltillo itself is an unlikely locale for any wildlife, as its complexion is industrial in nature, and the landscape is charmed by the likes of Kimberly-Clark's big Huggies plant at the city-limit marker. There is, however, in the center of town, a remarkable bird museum, aptly named the Museo de Aves, which has over 1,700 taxidermic representatives of more than 700 different species of the birds of Mexico. It is the home of the 40-year collection of Señor Aldegundo Garza de León and is now operated as a municipal museum. The dioramas were as professionally done as any we had ever

Colima Warbler (52), near Jama, Mexico, 1996

seen, and practically all of the birds of Mexico were on display, including the magnificent Harpy Eagle. A visit to this museum is well worth the trip from Monterrey to Saltillo, all by itself.

This time near Saltillo we did not work the low ground, but climbed to 9,000 feet into the deep oak and pine canyons south of the city in what are the Nieve Mountains of the Sierra Madre range. As we maneuvered through the elevations from 9,000 to 12,000 feet, passing through the villages of first Los Lireos and then later Jama, we moved out of the apple orchards of the valleys into the beautiful pine, spruce, madrona, and oak of the mountainside. On the side of this mountain, about six miles east of Jama, we found Colimas. The birds were not actively singing, and the ones we did find were in pairs. But find them we did, and after three active years of pursuit, we were finally able to get a picture of the Colima Warbler (no. 52). We saw quite a few birds over that two-day period, and we were able to get close enough to observe their behavior as well as their distinctive coloration. The

Colima Warbler, near Jama, Mexico, 1996

Colima is a large version of the Virginia's, certainly plain when compared to other warblers, but handsome in some respects. It is basically a gray bird, with a hard-to-see crown patch, but with rich yellow and amber orange in the rump region. When provoked, it will arch its tail over its back, almost wrenlike, and flash its colorful rump parts in a show of aggression. We were able to get some decent shots early, but recognizing full well that this was the last of the warblers we were pursuing, we kept at it, hoping for some "drop dead" photographs of this, our last warbler. When the weekend was over, and we had taken as many shots of the Colima as we were going to, Vera and I declared a final victory. We had ended with a splendid bird, and we could now lay claim to having taken photographs of all of the nonhybrid wood warblers that nest in the United States. All 52. Mission accomplished.

Finding the Colima Warbler concluded our quest to find all of the warblers, and although we took some pride in what we had accomplished, in our hearts a cold wind blew with the unsettling feeling that this kind of project might become problematic in not that many more years to come. Undoubtedly, many species of songbirds and warblers would continue to prosper in the future, but the more Vera and I delved into it, the more we observed, and the more we listened to others, the more firmly rooted has become our conviction that there is a real illness in the forests of the world and that our songbirds are clearly under siege. Where there had once been a swampy glade rich with wildlife, now a shopping center dominates the landscape; where there had once been a wild and remote mountain range, now mobile homes stalk the summit. The United States lost well over 300 million acres of its virgin forests during a 50-year period spanning the turn of the century, and more recently, acceptable nesting habitat for woodland songbirds has become more critically diminished each year. Not only are our warblers under great pressure here on their breeding grounds in North America, as their habitat has become sliced and fragmented; they are also more greatly stressed during migration with fewer and less adequate stopover points to rest and renourish. And finally, they are becoming increasingly destabilized on their wintering grounds in the tropics, as rainforests are slashed and burned for crop plots. Tanagers and flycatchers and thrushes are becoming harder to find in areas where they have always been, and grackles and starlings and cowbirds are comfortably moving in to take their place. Bird census counts, breeding bird surveys, and transect tabulations all point to the same conclusion: neotropical migrants are in serious trouble, and certain warbler populations are dropping alarmingly. The last time anyone saw a Bachman's Warbler was some 30 years ago in South Carolina, and it is now believed to be extinct, as its population was most likely irreversibly crippled by the destruction of its sole wintering range in the evergreen forests of Cuba. Also, the Kirtland's Warbler came within a whisker of extinction before habitat maintenance, controlled burning programs, and cowbird removal policies brought it back to some semblance of stabilized health. We know, however, that most of the trends are negative and that even if we do a good job in preserving habitat in this country, it is meaningless unless we are also able to save the birds' wintering grounds in the tropics. If we don't, there will most likely be birds that are pictured in our book today that will become extinct in our lifetime, and that the photographers who follow us won't have 52 to go after, but perhaps only 50, or 49, or fewer. We hope not, for the birds were the reason we embarked on our special journey in the first place. It was a good trip; we feel privileged to have been able to take it.

Postscript

WITH our long adventure over, Vera and I began to do other things on our weekends and to contemplate more civilized ways to spend vacation time than stalking warblers in rough terrain. We flirted with taking a cruise, or perhaps even a trip to Italy, which for years had been high on Vera's list. However, our first excursion in five to six years that wasn't designed around birds was a modest little trip to a marvelous former colonial town south of Mexico City called Oaxaca. We arrived several days after Christmas of 1996 and stayed in a 17th-century Dominican convent distinguished by its historical charm and Gregorian chants at breakfast.

We spent most of our time exploring the pre-Columbian ruins of the Olmec, Zapotec, and Mixtec civilizations, but after several days of full commitment to strictly tourist kinds of things, we began to check out the area for resident wildlife. We had brought a camera, "just in case," and early one morning Vera and I and our guide headed north of town about 45 minutes, and then climbed high into a cloud forest in the Cerro San Felipe near the small town of Yuvila. We wanted to look for the local birds in general but were specifically hoping to find the Red Warbler, a Mexican specialty known to be an inhabitant of the area. Off a dirt path running at the top of the mountain we found terrific habitat of usnea-covered live oaks, epiphytes, and several species of pine. We also found some splendid local birds of this highland area. But more importantly, we met the Red Warbler, a striking scarlet bird with a distinctive white cheek patch. As it moved up the side of the mountain, feeding low, we were actually able to get one decent picture of it. Its beauty served to punctuate the magnificence of the Mexican warblers, which in many instances have more vibrant colors than a great many of our own U.S. warblers.

Red Warbler, near Oaxaca, Mexico, 1997

And it was just then, after a deceptively casual discussion comparing the merits of both the U.S. and Mexican warblers, that Vera nonchalantly posed a question that had that disturbing and all-too-familiar ring: "Wouldn't it be fun to see how many Mexican warblers we . . . ?"

Bibliography

American Ornithologists' Union (AOU). 1957. *Check-list of North American Birds.*

Bartlett, Richard C. 1995. *Saving the Best of Texas.* Austin: University of Texas Press.

Bent, Arthur Cleveland. 1963. *Life Histories of North American Wood Warblers.* New York: Dover Publications.

Borror, Donald J., and William W. H. Gunn. 1985. *Songs of the Warblers of North America.* Cornell Laboratory of Ornithology, in association with the Federation of Ontario Naturalists.

Buckelew, Al, and George A. Hall. 1994. *The West Virginia Breeding Bird Atlas.* Pittsburgh: University of Pittsburgh Press.

Cody, Martin L. 1985. *Habitat Selection in Birds.* San Diego: Academic Press.

Curson, Jon, David Quinn, and David Beadle. 1994. *Warblers of the Americas.* New York and Boston: Houghton Mifflin Company.

Dennis, Jerry. 1996. *The Bird in the Waterfall.* New York: HarperCollins Publishers.

de Schauensee, Rudolphe Meyer, and William H. Phelps Jr. 1978. A *Guide to the Birds of Venezuela.* Princeton, N.J.: Princeton University Press.

Dunn, Jon L., and Eirik A. T. Blom (chief consultants). 1983. *A Field Guide to the Birds of North America.* Washington, D.C.: National Geographic Society.

Dunning, J. S., with the collaboration of Robert S. Ridgely. 1982. *South American Landbirds: A Photographic Guide to Identification.* Newton Square, Pa.: Harrowood Books.

Erickson, Laura. 1994. *For the Birds: An Uncommon Guide.* Duluth, Minn.: Pfeifer-Hamilton.

Garrett, K., and Jon L. Dunn. 1981. *Birds of Southern California: Status and Distribution*. Los Angeles: Los Angeles Audubon Society.

Griscom, Ludlow, and Alexander Sprunt Jr. 1979. *The Warblers of America*. Rev. ed. New York: Devin-Adair Company.

Harrison, George H. 1976. *Roger Tory Peterson's Dozen Birding Hot Spots*. New York: Simon and Schuster.

Harrison, Hal H. 1955. *American Birds in Color*. New York: William Wise Company.

———. 1984. *Wood Warblers' World*. New York: Simon and Schuster.

Hilty, Steven L. 1994. *Birds of Tropical America*. Shelbourne, Vt.: Chapters Publishing.

Hilty, Steven L., and William L. Brown. 1986. *Birds of Colombia*. Princeton, N.J.: Princeton University Press.

Holt, Harold R. 1989. *A Birder's Guide to Southeastern Arizona*. Colorado Springs: American Birding Association.

Knowler, Don. 1984. The Falconer of Central Park. Princeton, N.J.: Kanz-Cohl Publishers.

Lembke, Janet. 1992. *Dangerous Birds*. New York: Lyons and Burford.

McAlister, Wayne H., and Martha K. McAlister. 1993. *Matagorda Island: A Naturalist's Guide*. Austin: University of Texas Press.

Morse, Douglas H. 1989. *American Warblers*. Cambridge: Harvard University Press.

National Geographic Society. 1983. *Birds of North America*. Washington, D.C.

Neal, James A., and Joseph C. Neal. 1986. *Arkansas Birds*. Fayetteville: University of Arkansas Press.

Oberholser, Harry C. 1974. *The Bird Life of Texas*, vol. 2. Austin: University of Texas Press.

Peterson, Roger Tory. 1960. *A Field Guide to the Birds of Texas*. Boston: Houghton Mifflin Company.

Peterson, Roger Tory, and Edward L. Chalif. *A Field Guide to Mexican Birds*. 1973. Boston: Houghton Mifflin Company.

Phillips, Allan, Joe Marshall, and Gale Monson. 1964. *The Birds of Arizona*. Tucson: University of Arizona Press.

Porter, Eliot. 1972. *Birds of North America: A Personal Selection*. New York: E. P. Dutton and Company.

Pulich, Warren M. 1976. *The Golden-cheeked Warbler*. Austin: Texas Parks and Wildlife Department.

———. 1988. *The Birds of North Central Texas*. College Station: Texas A&M University Press.

Ridgely, Robert S. 1989. *A Field Guide to the Birds of Panama with Costa Rica, Nicaragua, and Honduras.* 2d ed. Princeton, N.J.: Princeton University Press.

Ridgely, Robert S., and Guy Tudor. 1989. *The Birds of South America.* Vol. 1, *The Oscine Passerines.* Austin: University of Texas Press.

Robbins, Chandler S., Bertel Brown, and Herbert S. Zim. 1966. *A Guide to Field Identification of Birds of North America.* New York: Golden Press.

———. 1983. *Birds of North America: A Guide to Field Identification.* New York: Western Publishing.

Salathe', T. 1991. *Conserving Migratory Birds.* Cambridge, England: International Council for Bird Preservation.

Skutch, Alexander F. 1954. "Family Parulidae." In *Life Histories of Central American Birds,* pp. 339–386. Pacific Coast Avifauna, no. 31. Berkeley, Calif.: Cooper Ornithological Society.

Snow, David W. 1976. *The Web of Adaptation.* Ithaca, N.Y.: Cornell University Press.

Stiles, F. Gary, and Alexander F. Skutch. 1989. *A Guide to the Birds of Costa Rica.* London: Christopher Helm.

Stokes, Don, and Lillian Stokes. 1996. *Field Guide to Birds.* Boston: Little, Brown & Company.

Terborgh, John W. 1980. "The Conservation Status of Neotropical Migrants: Present and Future." In *Migrant Birds in the Neotropics,* edited by Allen Keast and Eugene S. Morton, pp. 21–30. Washington, D.C.: Smithsonian Institution Press.

Terres, John K. 1980. *The Audubon Society Encyclopedia of North American Birds.* New York: Alfred A. Knopf.

Wauer, Roland H. 1973. *Birds of Big Bend National Park and Vicinity.* Austin: University of Texas Press.

Index

Boldface page numbers refer to photographs.